r 6/04

MAY 0 5

LOCAL AUTHOR DATE DUE

JUN 29 05

Violent Homeland

Other Works on Peace and Social Justice by Christopher Johnston

The Upādhi:
On Human Nature and the Nature of the Modern Human Experience, the Foundations of Peace and Social Justice

Sylvia Plath Was Murdered by The Murder Of Crows In My Head

Violent
Homeland

Christopher Johnston

Center for Alternative
Studies in Peace
and Social Justice

Johnston, Christopher
     Violent Homeland

ISBN: 1-59109-935-8

Data Cataloging:

1. Christopher Johnston   2. Poetry   3. Middle East Studies

Cover Art by Christopher Johnston:
     "Violent Homeland by Chris Johnston (a digitally altered
     reproduction of Pablo Picasso's *Guernica)* "

Published by Imprint Books in cooperation with the Center for
Alternative Studies in Peace and Social Justice

For Don Rhoades

Preface

I'm not Jewish and I'm not Christian and I'm not Sunni or Shi'a. I'm not British or Israeli or Turkish or Kurdish or Palestinian or Moroccan or Azeri; I'm not even from the Near or Middle East or for that matter Africa or for that matter Asia. I'm not a scholar of Near or Middle East politics or history or religion. I'm not a member of the U.N. or an N.G.O.

In almost every conceivable way, I am an outsider relative to the Near and Middle East–its land and institutions and people. I am an outsider, but for what it is worth here is what I think concerning the conflicts in the region: peace in the "homelands" is, if not all but impossible, a hell of a long way off. Because of current regional, national, and international political and geopolitical realities and the institutional structures associated with these realities, we will have at least a few hundred more years of what we have had for the last hundred or so.

The great-great-great-great-great grandchildren of the people that live on the dirt and sand that is generically called the Middle East are going to largely live the same lives as those living there now. Many people—hundreds, thousands, tens of thousands—are going to die violently between now and then, most of their names won't be remembered by anyone, not even their distant relatives. Kids with cute little button noses and big brown eyes are going to get blown to smithereens. Men and women, husbands and wives who ultimately just want to make a family together, are going to be shot in the head and bleed to death on the street in front of their houses. Girls who longingly wait to make their own home won't quite reach that day they have spent so many of their youthful hours dreaming about because they will be slowly rotting in the arid ground. Boys who just want to love God will be coldly murdered, most will call out their mother's name with their last breath. All these people are just going to be decomposed bodies, at least here on Earth (in the earth). I sincerely hope though they become something else (the something else they pray for) later.

I often think that most of these people–the ones already dead and those that are going to die sooner-or-later–have forgotten really important stuff about who and what they are, and perhaps most importantly, who they want to be. It's not their fault though, living with constant fear and loathing tends to make people's brains function poorly, tends to make people's minds extremely porous.

I may be an outsider, but I do know that today there is (just as there was yesterday and just as there will be tomorrow) a large handful of groups of people with pretty widely diverging conceptions of reality, the good, the beautiful, and what it means to be human vying for specific chunks of dirt and sand that they can inhabit and then on that soil lead a "good" life that directly corresponds with how they make sense of the universe and beyond. When you get right down to it, the ultimate goal of these people is merely to become fully realized human beings, to become whole, just like it is, in one way or another, the ultimate goal of every other human being on the planet.

It is a sad reality, but there are a lot of people in the world who are convinced that the only way they can become fully realized is to exterminate the people and institutions that they believe directly undermine and otherwise make impossible the process and/or goal of human wholeness as they understand it. I don't really understand what, for instance, suicide bombers are trying to accomplish with their actions apart from exacting revenge against their oppressors, although in their hearts I imagine they believe they are putting down their oppressors so that their brothers and sisters can be free to live the life they believe to be good and/or right and/or beautiful.

We inhabit a small planet with limited resources, conflicts are unavoidable, but when these conflicts escalate to armed conflict this process of becoming whole is obstructed in so many profound ways both obvious and subtle. The irony of the situation though is that violence for political gain is a highly effective means of procuring power, and it is the procurement of power that will likely lead to the establishment of homelands for these people to live and practice a good and/or right and/or beautiful life, a life of wholeness, ... but will this wholeness be possible?

Violence as a means to wholeness makes us less than who we are and who we are capable of being. It might even make wholeness impossible. In fact, I would bet that violence here cannot be a means to the desired end for these people. Further, and perhaps most importantly, violence as a means to wholeness makes us forget really important stuff, makes us ugly, very very ugly people. What's going on in the Middle East is particularly painful because the Muslims of Palestine and the Jews of Israel, the Kurds of Iraq, the Iranians, the Turks, and the Armenians, to name just a few of the antagonists, are such profoundly beautiful people, beautiful people that need, perhaps more than any other people on the face of the planet right now, to remember.

I have thought a whole lot about it, expended enormous amounts of time and mental energy on the matter, and I have come to the conclusion that I don't know shit about how to resolve any of the conflicts in the Near and Middle East, let alone solve the problems that underlie those conflicts. I'm not even all that sure what it is that I am trying to realistically accomplish with these words and phrases collected here, nothing of relevance has changed with regard to the conflicts since the birth of neocolonialism and regional nationalisms in the late Nineteenth Century and there is no reason to believe that anything will change in the future regardless of whether I add my thoughts and ideas to the conversation or not. I guess my hope though is that this integrated collection of thoughts and ideas on the matter will help those involved in the conflicts to remember who they want to be, and too to see who they have become, which I believe is very distant from who they want to be.

Now I certainly don't begrudge any of the antagonists their dream of a home and self-determination within its walls, and I concede that murdering Hadef and Aaron and Sadia and Tadeo and Robert and Golda and Naisha and Amy and Ian and Henda and Abdullah and Kenneth and Kapel and Afet and Sirvat and Elizabeth will likely get the killers this refuge. My concern though is that it will all be for not later, and by "later" I mean "forever starting tomorrow."

Christopher Johnston, 2002

Violent Homeland

Palestine et al.

His fingers scratch gestures of loneliness across my back;
he cannot press his hands against me, . . .
and he will try to laugh.

Surrounded by a tranquility specific only to her,
she pleasures my body with repetetive restitutions to the devine;
the promises of perfection made to the face written in my soul
escape the desolation left raped across her bodies.

Their body is the madness
and in the hands of invisible torturers,
forsaken by their careless caresses
and fluent wounds left open
so as to obfuscate heaven.

Untitled 4

I fear my body moves and is directionless;
I fear the sand passing my time.

     I am no witness to any memory that could have been a weapon used to murder someone other than my own history which is, as I have said and dreamed so many times, only the whisper of something dark and not mine at all.

Jews, Christians, Muslims, and Picasso's Brooding Woman (1904)

The obviousness of your soul is compensated for by a delicacy
        and fluency that you will not admit to.
Your brooding extreme is in opposition to the world you
        imprison in your bitter head,
a generally accepted symbolism that begins and ends and then
        disappears.

A thin skin of light is all that brings continuity to your blue exterior,
a stain that simultaneously defines and destroys you.

I close my eyes and wonder if there is really somebody there,
staring by you,
or if blots are just blots
and stains just stains, isolation real or implied;
I wonder if you are more than just stylistic extremes.

By agreement in someone else's head you are unchangeable,
all your faces accepted without execution and sentiment,
your ample breasts accepted without oversimplification.
Your body should have been more than an experiment,
more than a commentary,
but you could imagine it in no other way.

The Aftermath

There is contradiction in my breathing,
I am aware of its many crazy faces—contorted mouth and
       misshapen noses and misplaced eyes.
I am having trouble breathing,
my chest feels too small.

Apart from the dead and bloody dove in my pocket,
I have no friend.
Apart from the forgetfulness,
I am without change, my mind and body and soul little more
       than a statue ….
You made me this way …
with your crazy faces:

It was a furious passion that made me your animal,
a complex and profound kiss that could only be read like a novel,
the touch of your yellow fingers that smelled like stale cigarettes
       but were otherwise gentle.

I was too young to have memories or complete thoughts,
I did not yet have a functioning voice,
my eyes did not yet tell of oblivion,
but you still encircled me as if I had and was all these things,
you still worshiped me with your great heart,
and because of the vast greatness of your heart I came to see
       with your eyes
and believe to be true that which they saw.

I Remain Unmoved,

venturing on, not pushing forward.

> *Since her return I have been asleep*
> *I am unafraid,*
> *without shape,*
> *nocturnal.*

Slowly I wander, never going, never arriving;
time passes slowly through my hour-glass mouth.

> *Her new smile slips through/from her face,*
> *slips ... slowly ... through/from her face.*

As if it were a history of droughts and storms,
this narrative scribbled into your head is locally unpredictable,
but with a destiny that is globally stable.

A moment suddenly uncontainable,
time defiling my essence as it explodes, gains speed,
reaches a place of no time,
a place where time cannot exist,
nor wants to.

> *Her new smile slips through/from her face*
> *without shape,*
> *a mouth without good words.*

> The dead lie on the ground,
> deeply asleep.

Breathing, …

flat…. I think I can remember you:

> I was a man, many men, and … ,
> and the sun had stopped;
> I think I can remove you,
> but you are fragile,
> except when . . . ,
> when you were a little girl
> and … ,
> and when you were a river, …
> long before you were this or any other poem.

Beautiful Traveler

She waits for my love and sanity to fill her—
one she winds around her head tightly,
one she fashions into a halo,
one she can wear on a chain around her neck.

She can dream herself a butterfly,
and altogether contingent,
a masterpiece of suffering
overflowing with burdens
I cannot even begin to fashion with beautiful words.

Incapable of being with clarity,
she is easily extinguished
despite a boundlessness that is easily palpable,
despite the ability to receive into her soul the earthquakes
*   originating from my heart.*

But there is a cruelness too:
she has the power to transform the heavens at will—
move Rigel to Tayamnituchuhu to beta Orionis—
and breathe life into statues of wood, and statues of clay.
I would be lying if I said I did not love this,
but too I am frightened by her obtuse disrespect.

Beautiful traveler, omnipresent guide,
barefoot I walk the road of you,
at night I rise and dance with memories of you,
but I do not expect you to remember me,
or even the little names you gave me so long ago, …
only to replenish you when you are asleep next to another
who is, to you, nothing but an unwitting diversion
from the life you are too frightened to live.

"OH POO!", Mrs. Tanner stammers, her arthritic hands fumbling with the small white child-resistant cap she is trying to replace.

She puts the bottle down next to the tall bottle on the sink counter and then sets the cap on top of it. She steps back and looks at the line-up: a clear bottle with a semi-transparent red label, a blue bottle, an opaque yellow bottle with a yellow cap, a little short bottle, a bottle that is smoke brown, another that is disproportionately fat, one has square corners, another is purple, a bottle that is burnt orange, a bottle that is tall, one that is very old and has a hand written prescription label hiding its contents, a bright pink bottle, a big bottle that could almost be called a jar, and finally a green bottle with sugar pills in it (at least that's what she thinks they are).

Mrs. Tanner picks up the blue bottle and puts it next to the wall. She sets the brown next to it and then the yellow, the clear, the orange, the old, the purple, the fat, the tall, the square, the short, the pink, the green, and then the big bottle that could almost be called a jar goes at the end. She wrinkles her nose and switches the tall with the short, the yellow with the old, the pink with the brown, the purple goes to the end next to the big, the fat with the yellow, and the blue goes in the slot where the purple was.

Mr. Tanner, God rest his soul, used to look at the row of bottles, shake his head with disgust, and call his wife a hypochondriac. Sometimes when he had a few too many boubons he would even call her a hypochondriac bitch. ("Bourbon" was not in his vocabulary, only "bourbons.")

Mrs. Tanner looks in the mirror above the sink, beyond the mascara and rouge and lipstick, beyond the coverup and foundation, beyond the wrinkles and long ago faded bruises; she sees an old face. She leans closer to the mirror, she thinks she sees the eyes of a lonely woman struggling not to be forgotten, but maybe not, the image is fleeting.

Mrs. Tanner looks at the row of pills again, reaches out

and switches the clear with the pink, the green with the old, the short one with the tall one, the yellow with the square, blue with the orange and then the orange with the fat, the square with the pink, and the clear she picks up and squishes in the space between the big and the purple.

"Now Mrs. Tanner, what are you going to do with yourself?" she giggles. She picks up the bottle next to the wall and with great difficulty takes the cap off. She pours a dozen or so pills into her gnarled hand and then pops them all into her mouth. "Silly girl," she mumbles through the jumble of pills. She laughs and before she can get the glass of bourbon to her lips a few of the pills fall out of her mouth and bounce off the counter onto the floor.

She thinks about putting the fat bottle in the old bottle's spot and then the green in the fat's, but decides instead to take a nap, maybe read a little bit first. Her daughter sent her a book of poetry last week; inside the front cover her daughter wrote:

love you,

M

The Legacy

Of he who has seen everything, I will make known to all of you.
I will teach of he who has experienced all things,
near and far alike,
Anu granted him the totality of knowledge.
He saw the Secret, discovered the Mystery and Hidden,
he brought stories and knowledge of the time before the Flood.
He went on a great journey, pushing himself beyond exhaustion,
but then he was brought to peace.
He carved his story on stone tablets,
and built the great and mighty wall of Uruk-Haven,
the wall of the sacred Eanna Temple, the holy sanctuary.
Look at this wall, the likes of which no one has ever equaled!
Take hold of the threshold stone—it comes from ancient times!
Go close to the Eanna Temple, the residence of Ishtar,
such as no later king or man ever equaled!
Go up on the wall of Uruk and walk,
inspect its foundation, examine its brickwork thoroughly.
Is not even the core of the brick structure made of kiln-fired brick,
and did not the Seven Sages themselves lay out its plans?
One league city, one league palm gardens, one league lowlands, the
open area of the Ishtar Temple,
three leagues and the open area of Uruk the wall encloses.

Find the copper tablet box,
open the hasp of its lock of bronze,
undo the fastening of its secret opening.
Take and read out loud from the lapis lazuli tablet
how Gilgamesh went through every hardship. …

Fully Interpreted Life

Senility locked deeply in my head,
there is no resistance, your thoughts
push me back,
pinning me up against the wall,
your hand completely covering my mouth
and heart.

Across my lips and eyes I feel your dry implied history blow,
I think I hear old names and dark I love you's,
I remember your fully interpreted life
and remember it sweet and delicious.

Falling into your sacramental arms,
amid the multitude of enemy angels without eyes
I lay, inanimate and without substance,
overflowing with a nothingness
that I can no longer remain submerged in.

Gilgamesh

… Supreme over other kings,
lordly in appearance,
Gilgamesh is the hero, born of Uruk, the goring wild bull.
He walks out in front, the leader,
and walks at the rear, trusted by his companions.
Mighty shield, protector of his people,
raging flood-wave who destroys even walls of stone!
Son of Lugalbanda, Gilgamesh is strong to perfection,
son of the august cow, Rimat-Ninsun,
unlike all other mortals, Gilgamesh is awesome to perfection.

It was Gilgamesh who opened the mountain passes,
who dug wells on the side of the mountain.
It was he who crossed the ocean, the vast seas to the rising sun,
who explored the whole of the world, seeking life.
It was he who reached by his own sheer strength of character
            and body Utanapishtim, the Faraway,
who restored the cities that the flood destroyed!

There has never been as great a manking.
Who can compare with him in kingliness?
Who can say like Gilgamesh: "I am King!"?
Whose name, from the day of his birth, was called "Gilgamesh"?
Two-thirds of him is god, one-third of him human.
The Great Goddess Aruru fashioned the form of his body,
she prepared him from the best things
so that he would be beautiful, the handsomest of men,
his body and face perfect,
his mind cunning and his heart brave to perfection.

He walks around in the enclosure of Uruk,
like a wild bull he makes himself mighty, head raised above
            all others.

There is no rival who can raise a weapon against him.
His men stand at the ready, ready to carry out his orders,
he is their respected king.

But the men of Uruk become anxious in his presence,
Gilgamesh does not leave a son to his father,
day and night he arrogantly tests every man and boy to prove
       his own greatness.
In Gilgamesh the shepherd of Uruk-Haven,
there is no peace, he is the shepherd
trusted but feared,
bold, eminent, knowing, wise,
two-thirds god, one third man,
he is alone.

Gilgamesh does not leave a girl to her betrothed!
The daughter of the warrior, the bride of the young man,
the gods kept hearing their complaints,
so the gods of the heavens implored Anu:
       "You have brought into being a mighty wild bull,
       head raised above all others!
       There is no rival who can raise a weapon against him.
       Gilgamesh does not leave a son to his father,
       day and night he arrogantly tests every man and boy to
           prove his own greatness.
       In Gilgamesh the shepherd of Uruk-Haven,
       there is no peace, he is the shepherd
       trusted but feared,
       bold, eminent, knowing, wise,
       two-thirds god, one third man,
       he is alone.
       Gilgamesh does not leave a girl to her betrothed! …

The Other

Pretending your isolation,
drifting in and out of me,
gray and sullen and secret with obscenity.

You scribble a sacramental plagiarism onto scraps of paper you
        put in your pocket, ... and forget about.

Walking back, out of your past,
my feet hardly touching the ground,
but leaving deep scars in the dust that you will tell your next
        lover about.
        And he will be sympathetic and tell you he loves
you and you will believe him like you believed me when
everything was exactly as it is now ... except for the face
he wears was mine.

        Without knowing, he will devote himself to the
stagnation gnawing away at your memory, the memories of
you holding my eternity in the challis of your little hands,
an unwitting witness to life's proclamations writ large in an
absurdity eager to manufacture your truth of heaven.

Overwhelmed by the demands of ecstasy,
he too will wander through his life crippled,
an abstraction drowning in the water metaphors that flow freely
        from your liquid mouth.

The Panther By
Rainer Maria Rilke

It is his body, the way that he throws himself across the cage,
the reckless abandon with which he in one moment exists,
and then in the next is no longer.

It is as if he is an animal,
a panther,
scratching the passing of each day into the concrete wall
so as to never completely forget.

Without even looking I know when he is holding his
hand out, lending me support.

His old frail hands tremble before me as if he is
incanting a spell across me. There is a cross burned into his
forehead. As if by magic, I am immediately self aware—I can
feel the warmth of the dawn rising over me, these long, unbroken
curves, Heaven perhaps.

It is his eyes that worry me and bring me to
tears—everything and nothing filling them simultaneously. He
is little more than the shell of the animal that he should
be. When I close my eyes I realize that everything is so
unclear, every hope and false hope. I realize that every
whisper, itself an entity, one wrapped in prosaic swaddling
clothing—complex screams.

He wraps himself around me, sometimes quickly,
sometimes slowly. He knows that I am watching and know
everything, but does not care, his mind filled with abstractions
that he will never comprehend. When he thinks that I am
not looking, he gently runs his hand down the bars as if
they were a woman. He somehow knows that I am not afraid
to touch him like that.
The moments of peace I hold in my hand

are improperly put together,
waiting for a whisper,
to bury that whisper in my head, in the screaming that defines the
dimensionless line between my mind and not my mind.

All alone in a crowd:
and I fall down.

It is as if he is drunk, stumbling across the cold concrete floor,
stepping in his own excrement over and over again.

And there . . . . the beautiful.

Seduced into a child's voice,
our fates once equal
now grow, with each breath, disparate.

Across my face I scratch a thousand marks with the thousand
fingers with sharp nails on my right and left hands.

She says she gives away her beauty;
"I am for you," she says.
She says she is an abyss for me to fill.

I can hold you tightly, permanently,
but let you go ...
to sleep.

Strange
man
seeking
asylum,
crazy man
without ears.

His vision from the passing of the bars
is grown so weary that it holds no more.
To him it seems there are a thousand bars
and behind a thousand bars no world.
The padding gait of flexibly strong strides,
that in the very smallest circle turns,
is like a dance of strength around a center
in which stupefied a great will stands.

Only sometimes the curtain of the pupil
soundlessly parts—. Then an image enters,
goes through the tensioned stillness of the limbs—
and in the heart ceases to be.

My mind is a desert,
living in dreams.

Enkidu

… The daughter of the warrior, the bride of the young man,
Anu listened to their complaints,
and the gods called out to Aruru:
> "It was you, Aruru, who created Gilgamesh
> now create a diversion for him.
> Let him be equal to Gilgamesh's tempestuous heart,
> let them be a match for each other so that Uruk may find
> > peace in their peace!"

When Aruru heard this she created within herself the answer
> to Anu.
Aruru washed her hands, she pinched off some clay, and threw
> it into the wilderness.

There, in the wild grew the valiant Enkidu,
born of silence, endowed with strength by Ninurta.
His whole body was covered with shaggy hair,
he had a full head of hair like a woman,
his locks billowed in profusion like Ashnan.
He knew neither people nor settled living,
but wore a loincloth like Sumukan.
He grazed with the gazelles,
and played at the watering hole with the animals;
as with animals, his thirst was sated with mere water. …

Falling

I have, my whole life, been falling,
tumbling unobstructed into the shadows,
absorbing the cold and silence through my porous skin,
my eyes, no longer necessary, becoming only a memory
like my heart.

I no longer know if I am of substance,
if I am of time.

My mind is composed wholly of fatigue,
no more love, no more hunger, no more God or gods,
no more dreams,
no dreams of love and hunger and God and gods,
no wondering if people mourn for me or tell stories about me.
I can no longer think, ... just believe,
... and I believe now ... in the cold and silence,
in the darkness that is wet with tears wept for those that believe,
knowing that death will never find them here,
life couldn't ... or didn't want to.

Exactitude is Not Truth to Painters or Ghosts, Just to God

My mind is easily ignored,
an object in appearance only,
a sea of inherent truths disengaged from the outward appearance
        that is neither organic nor true.
Ripeness.
Wholeness.
Vulnerability.
God.

The material devours my hand before I can finish painting,
it has always been inevitable,
subconscious confusion beyond my own genetic evolution
or any justification that might be interpreted as fundamental.

My primitive mouth.
My incomplete face,
my disintegrating spiritual body overwhelmed by your own
        mythical madness.
It is the passage of servile time,
a flowing legend without clarity of vision or sensitivity.
His (my) head has no geographical destiny,
no future of love or loving, suffocating or not.
Scattered.
Nothing.
Forgotten.

Boys
And Girls
And Old Words With New Meanings

He stands,
stares,
mouth a silhouette.

He is nineteen and already so tired.

He just says that he is cold ...
and that he wishes he could make tears.

He falls off the edge of the world,
then there is silence,
then he spins wildly off into the heavens.
He cries out that he is dizzy ... and that he thinks he is going
       to be sick.
Very few people hear him,
and none that understand the tongue with which he feels
       compelled to use.

He looks into the eyes of the others spinning off in tangents
       to himself,
he does not recognize his own eyes inserted into their faces,
or that the fear lipsticked onto their lips is his own
... or virtually indistinguishable from it.

He thinks that he no longer understands regret,
that only God can understand the truth about him. Certainty, now,
is his own private defeat.

[he writes on a piece of paper:]
There must be some way out of here,
I walk in circles,

scribble my name into the fine dirt,
it cannot resist my dominion … or my mind which turns it into
       pure water.

• • •

The history-tumors that grow in her are not alive, but the living.
I can smell them in her sweat, taste them in her saliva, feel them
racing around on her skin.
       Faithfully to my body you pray,
       naked girl full of obscure writing,
       I am the pulse of your pen,
       I dream and then am alive with your words,
       confused symbols that cannot share the same dimension,
       inaccessible even with really long arms—
           I hear her as the light fades away,
           before I go to sleep at night.

       Maybe she doesn't love me, maybe she does not
know who I am, maybe this desolate space carved from the
gray matter in my head is not the heaven she pretends it
to be. She stands,
       stares,
       mouth a silhouette.

Watchers look away, easing the pain burning her eyes.
Maybe-lovers cry for her beauty to return.
Wrists slashed with empathy bleed into the ground like lovers
       into the arms of lovers.

She offers her communion-breast to his mouth,
but it is dry with the desert grotesquely slipping its tongue in
       and out of her mouth.

He kisses her wrists and says goodbye.

She spins violently off into someone else's heaven.

She says she has forgotten the drama of the pain,

She melts into history like a whore into the darkness of
an other:

Old Words With New Meanings is essentially a story about a man in his mid-thirties, call him E, who one morning meets a woman of maybe twenty-one or twenty-two years, call her S, in a park. They strike up a conversation that ends up lasting about twenty-four hours.

There is essentially no script for the screenplay, and very few "stage" directions. The idea is to take two actors and give them a set of initial conditions in the form of character profiles and a guide of sorts as to how the day will unfold, and then capture that whole day on film. Essentially, the approach in filming should more closely approximate that of a documentary rather than a feature, although it is most accurate to see it as something of a hybrid between the two.

There should be little rehearsal and no interaction between the actors playing E and S before the cameras begin to roll. In fact, they should not even know what the other looks like until E walks over to S and strikes up a conversation. For this reason, there should be a considerable amount of effort put into trying to cast two actors that will find each other attractive.

As mentioned, the day begins in a park, the park bordering a large body of water, perhaps the Puget Sound of Seattle, the Bay of San Francisco, or the Columbia River of Portland. The two are drinking coffee from Styrofoam cups and staring out into the water, E sitting on a bench and S not too far away leaning up against a railing.

E stands up and walks away in the direction of S. He has noticed her, but has paid little attention to her. She, on the other hand has not seen him, given that he was sitting on a bench behind her. As he reaches the point at which he will pass S he slows to a stop, thinks for a moment, and then walks to the railing a couple of feet from her.

E says good morning, and S, after a moment of trepidation, smiles and says good morning back...; the conversation has begun, a conversation that the actors, with but a few small exceptions, improvise. The conversation can go anywhere the actors want to take it, but should be dominated by stories of themselves. These stories are grounded in the character profiles provided, although the character profiles are largely taken from the lives of the actors themselves after casting. That is to say, there are some very important events that each of the characters has lived through, events that molded their lives in incalculable ways. These events are offered in the character profiles. All of the gaps, however, are filled in with the personal experiences of the actor portraying either E or S. The trick then is for the actors to blend the fictitious events of E and S's life into their own memories such that they indeed become, for all practical purposes, part of their own past and thereby can speak of them fluently and within a context.

Back to the story: S, although a gentle woman, is obviously the more dominant personality. E is the follower. Actually, all that E really seems to want to do on this particular day is spend it with S, follow her around, if you will; S is more than happy to allow this, and in fact, is quite happy to have the company.

The day in conversation is spent wandering around the city. They perhaps find themselves walking through the park, perhaps through a zoo, maybe too a museum, certainly a bridal store where S tries on wedding dresses, and possibly they ride around a bit on public transportation and explore a smelly old used bookstore and roam through an open air market and whatever; whatever the city in which it is filmed lends itself to is fair game for the backgrounds of their conversation.

In order to maintain at least some semblance of spontaneity in this more-or-less controlled setting only the actor portraying S should be aware of the journey they will take—the places they will go to and the things they will do. Really, the only thing the actor portraying E needs to know about most of the daytime wandering about is that he is to go along with S.

The sun low in the sky, S and E find themselves in front of the apartment building in which S lives. There is a brief moment of hesitation on S's part before she invites E in for a bite to eat. Similarly, there is a moment of hesitation on E's part before he accepts.

This section, although only a small portion of the total film, is scripted, albeit loosely, and not much more instructive or revealing than what is to follow here.

S's apartment is a funky little thing, immaculately kept, and inviting like no home E has ever seen or been in.

S prepares dinner and E sets the table at which they then devour their creation over a bottle or two of wine.

After dinner, E washes the dishes and S cleans up and dries. When finished, S lights a few candles and then turns off the lights. E empties the wine bottle into their glasses evenly and then carries them to a coffee table in front of the sofa. The two sit down very close to each other. They talk softly, but add the dimension of touching, of playing with each other's hands.

Within a very short period of time they are gently and tentatively kissing and caressing. This leads to a more passionate encounter where eventually they succumb to their pent up hungers and desires, virtually ripping each others clothes off.

Foreplay is passionate, but brief. S gently but forcefully pushes E to the floor and straddles him. She continues to kiss and bite, and tease, but after only a minute or two of this she brings it all to an abrupt halt. Her reason? She is ready to bring him into her. There is much adjusting on S's part, and much frustration. Intercourse just isn't going to happen.

The closer they approach intercourse the more guarded E grows until that impossible point where S tries to lower herself onto him. He cannot do it. Gently he tries to push S away, but she is determined. He is a little more forceful, but again, S will not relent, not until E begins sobbing.

Confused, S rises up off of E and then moves around to comfort him. She takes his head into her lap, softly whispering healing words to him. His sobbing slowly modulates into mere weeping.

After some time, E, weak from crying, pulls himself up off the floor and puts his pants on. S has already risen and is in the kitchen readying two mugs for tea; she is wearing his shirt.

E, a blanket draped over his naked shoulders, walks out onto the little balcony and stares out into the stars. S brings the tea out and the two stand tightly together, drinking and peering silently out into the heavens.

E eventually tries to apologize, but S hushes him with a gentle finger placed perfectly across his lips. They grow silent again until S suggests that they take a bath. E concurs. S leaves the balcony to fill the tub, E turns back to the stars until he is called into the bathroom.

S is already in the big tub when E gets there, she mostly hidden under a thick sheet of bubbles. E takes his pants off and climbs in, she enfolds him in her arms and legs. He leans back into her and closes his eyes.

After a while, the sheet of bubbles now thin, S begins to wash E with a cloth. She is also exploring his body, this being the first time she has seen him naked in adequate light. She works her way across his back and chest and arms, trying not to be to sensual, although sensual enough.

Almost done, she abruptly stops at his wrists and hands. She washes the suds away as best she can. There, across his wrists, are deep scars, two on each wrist. They are healed but not yet worn smooth with time. She gently traces them with her finger nail and then with the pad of her finger tip.

E watches her somewhat nervously, but says nothing.

Over and over she traces the scars until finally she takes his left hand in both of her hands and raises his wrist to her lips. There is a prominent band of white skin where his wedding ring had been up until a couple of days ago. S briefly touches the band with her own finger. She turns her attentions to his wrists where she slowly runs her tongue over the scars several times before softly kissing them; she also kisses the place where his wedding band had been.

S puts E's hand down and then takes the other, raising it to her lips, running her tongue across the scars on his wrists and then kissing them.

She puts his hand back down into the water and after a few awkward moments raises her own hand up out of the water and holds it in front of E's eyes. There on her wrist are two scars, each equally as nasty and as new as his own.

E stares at them until her hand begins to tremble. He gently takes her hand in his, kisses the scars on her wrists, and then draws it tightly to his chest. E closes his eyes and leans back into S who again enfolds him in her arms and legs.

Sometime later, the two are lying naked on top of S's bed. They are caressing and kissing. There is no mad passion between them, just a simple and beautiful tenderness.

Eventually the two do make love, or, perhaps more accurately, they share an emotionally intimate union, and then fall deeply asleep in each other's arms.

Several hours later, the room blooming in the light of the morning sun, S awakens. She yawns and rubs the sleep out of her eyes.

E is dressed and stands leaning up against the bedroom door jam. He is smiling, but his eyes are sad.

S too is smiling, and too it is a sad smile.

They tightly hold each others stare for a seemingly very long time, each knows there are no more words left to share.

E silently backs out of the room.

S stares at the doorway where E had stood until she hears the front door close. She rolls over onto her side and notices the four crisp one hundred dollar bills bent and standing on edge atop the night stand. In the cup of the bent bills is a fifth bill, one folded into an origami swan.

S contorts herself around to pick up the bills. She takes them, counts them, and sets all but the folded one in a convenient place on the bed or pillow. The swan she closely examines, smiling softly. After a few moments she puts the swan with the other bills, rolls over, cuddles up with the pillow E had been using and goes back to sleep.

242 & 242 Revisited

My destinies drift into existence silently,
someone else's heart ripped from their chest
round and around with dark red sacrilege,
almost black with your profanity
dawning at the feet of one or another god.

• • •

I am a child walking on water
with feet that are not my own.

Obscure Writing

It is a transformational inertia that stands erect before him as if a
        monument,
an intrinsic history marginalized behind revisionist antagonisms
        and repetitions.
There is a unique method to his consciousness,
one measured in broken glass
and concrete rubble;
there is a unique method to everything he thinks ... and rethinks.

Obscure:

> "The day came when my release from the profession of
> rhetoric was to become a reality, just as, in my mind, I
> was free from it already. The deed was done, and you
> rescued my tongue, as you had already rescued my heart.
> Praising you and full of joy I set out for the house in the
> country with all my friends and relations. Once we were
> there I began at last to serve you with my pen. The books
> I wrote are evidence of this, although the old air can still
> be sensed in them, as though I were still panting from
> my exertions in the school of pride. In them are recorded
> the discussions I held with my friends who were with me
> and my deliberations with myself when I was alone in
> your presence; and my correspondence with Nebridius,
> who was not with us, can still be read in my letters. But
> time could never suffice for me to set down on paper
> all the great blessings which you bestowed upon me,
> particularly at that time, since I must hurry on to tell of
> greater things.
>
>   For I remember the kind of man I was, 0 Lord, and it
> is a sweet task to confess how you tamed me by pricking
> my heart with your goad; how you *bridged every valley,*
> *levelled every mountain and hill* of my thoughts; how
> you *cut straight their windings, paved their rough paths;*

and how you also brought Alypius, whom in my heart I regarded as a brother, to submit to the name of your only-begotten Son, our Lord and Saviour Jesus Christ. At first he thought this unworthy of mention in my books, because he wanted them to carry the scholarly fragrance of the *cedars of Lebanon, which the Lord has now broken,* rather than that of the herbs with which the Church heals the bites of serpents.

How I cried out to you, my God, when I read the Psalms of David, those hymns of faith, those songs of a pious heart in which the spirit of pride can find no place! I was new to your true love. I was a catechumen living at leisure in that country house with Alypius, a catechumen like myself, and my mother, who never left us. She had the weak body of a woman but the strong faith of a man, the composure of her years, a mother's love for her son, and the devotion of a Christian. How I cried out to you when I read those Psalms! How they set me on fire with love of you! I was burning to echo them to all the world, if only I could, so that they might vanquish man's pride. And indeed they are sung throughout the world and just as none can hide away from the sun *none can escape your burning* heats. The thought of the Manichees filled me with angry resentment and bitter sorrow, yet I pitied them too, because in their ignorance of the sacraments that heal us they raved against the very remedy that could have cured them of their madness. I wished that they could have been somewhere at hand, unknown to me, to watch my face and hear my voice as I read the fourth Psalm. They would have seen how deeply it moved me. *When I call on your name, listen to mine,* 0 *God, and grant redress; still, in time of trouble, you have brought me relief; have pity on me now, and hear my prayer.* How I wish that they could have heard me speak these words!

And how I wish that I might have been unaware that they could hear, so that they need have no cause to think that my own words, which escaped from me as I recited the Psalm, were uttered for their benefit alone and it is true enough that I would not have uttered them, or if I had, I should not have uttered them in the same way, if I had known that they were watching and listening. And if I had uttered them, the Manichees would not have understood them in the way that I spoke them. They would not have understood how this cry came from my inmost heart, when I was alone in your presence.

I quivered with fear, yet at the same time I was aglow with hope, rejoicing in your mercy, my Father. All these emotions were revealed in the light of my eyes and the tremor of my voice, when I read the message of your Holy Spirit: *Great ones of the world, will your hearts always be hardened, will you never cease setting your heart on shadows, following a lie?* For it was just this that I had done. But you, 0 Lord, had already raised your holy Son to glory. You had *raised him from the dead and bidden him sit on your right hand,* so that from his place at your side he might send us the one whom he had promised, the Paraclete, *the truth giving Spirit.* He had already sent the Paraclete and I had not known it. He had already risen from the dead and ascended into heaven. He had already been raised to glory, and because of this he had sent the Paraclete. *The Spirit had not yet been given to siren, because Jesus had not yet been raised to glory.* But the words of the prophet are loud in our ears: *Will your hearts always be hardened, will you never cease setting your heart on shadows, following a lie? Be sure* of this, that the Lord has raised his holy Son to glory. The words are loud in our ears *"Will your hearts always be hardened? Be sure"* and yet, for so long, I had not known their meaning. I had set my heart on shadows and followed a lie, and this was why I was frightened when I heard these words, because I remembered that I had been just such a man as those to whom they are spoken. For there had been shadows and lies in the phantasms which I had taken for the truth, and the memory of my past wrung many loud cries of sorrow from my lips. How I wish that my cries could have been heard by those who still set their hearts on shadows and followed lies! Perhaps they would have been made to feel the error of their ways and would have disgorged it like vomit. And you would have heard them when they cried out to you, for Christ, who pleads with you for us, truly died for us in the flesh.

I read on: *Tremble and sin no more,* and this moved me deeply, my God, because by now I had learnt to tremble for my past, so that in future I might sin no more. And it was right that I should tremble, because it was not some other nature belonging to the tribe of darkness that had sinned in me, as the Manichees pretend. They do not tremble, but *they store up retribution for themselves against the day of retribution, when God will reveal the justice of his judgements.*

The good which I now sought was not outside myself. I did not look for it in things which are seen with the eye of the flesh by the light of the sun. For those who try to find joy in things outside themselves easily vanish away into emptiness. They waste themselves on the temporal pleasures of the visible world. Their minds are starved and they nibble at empty shadows. How I wish that they would tire of going hungry and cry out for a sight of better times! This is the answer they would hear from us: *Already, Lord, the sunshine of your favour has been plainly shown to us.* For we are not ourselves the Light which enlightens every soul. We are enlightened by you, so that we who *once were all darkness* may now, *in the Lord, be all daylight.* How I wish that they could see the eternal light within us! Now that I had glimpsed it myself I fretted and chafed because I could not make them see it. For if they had come to me and *cried out for a sight of better times,* I should have seen that their hearts looked out through their eyes on the world outside, away from you. But it was in my inmost heart, where I had grown angry with myself, where I had been stung with remorse, where I had slain my old self and offered it in sacrifice, where I had first purposed to renew my life and had placed my hope in you, it was there that you had begun to make me love you and had *made me glad at heart.* It was my eyes that read these words but my soul that knew their meaning. They brought a cry to my lips and I wished no more for the manifold riches of this earth, things on which I should lose time, only to be lost in time myself. For in eternity, which is one alone, I had other *corn and wine and oil.*

When I read the next verse, a loud cry broke from my heart. *In peace and friendliness I will sleep; I will take my rest* in the eternal God. 0, the joy of these words! For, *when the saying of Scripture comes true, and death is swallowed up in victory,* who shall withstand us? You truly are the eternal God, because in you there is no change and in you we find the rest that banishes all our labour. For there is no other besides you and we need not struggle for other things that are not what you are, and it was you, 0 Lord, who *bade me repose in confidence unprotected.*

I read the Psalm and there was fire in my heart, but I could think of no means of helping those deaf corpses, of whom I had myself been one. For I had been evil as the plague. Like a cur I had snarled blindly and bitterly against the Scriptures, which are sweet with the honey of heaven and radiant with your light. And now *I was sick at heart over the rebellion* of those who hate them.

When shall I set down the record of those days of rest? One thing at least I shall not fail to tell, for I have not forgotten the sting of your lash nor how quickly your mercy came, and in how wonderful a way. During that vacation you let me suffer the agony of toothache, and when the pain became so great that I could not speak, my heart prompted me to ask all my friends who were with me to pray to you for me, since you are the God who gives health to the body as well as to the soul. I wrote down the message and gave it to them to read, and as soon as we knelt down to offer you this humble prayer, the pain vanished. What was that pain? How did it vanish? My Lord and my God, I confess that I was terrified, for nothing like this had ever happened to me in all my life. Deep within me I recognized the working of your will and I praised your name, rejoicing in my faith. But my faith would not let me feel at ease over my past sins, for they had not yet been forgiven in your baptism."

Saint Augustine

The Trapper And The Harlot

… A well-known trapper
came face-to-face with Enkidu opposite the watering hole.
A first, a second, and a third day
he came face-to-face with him opposite the watering hole.
On seeing Enkidu the trapper's face flushed with fear,
and Enkidu and the animals drew back and ran away.
He was rigid with fear; though motionless
his face looked like one who had made a long journey.

The trapper addressed his father:
"Father, a strange man has come from the mountains.
He is mightiest in the land,
his strength is as mighty as the Meteorite of Anu!
He went over the mountains,
he played at the watering hole with the animals,
he stands opposite the watering hole.
I was afraid, so I did not go up to him.
He filled in the pits that I had dug,
wrenched out my traps that I had spread,
released from my grasp the wild animals.
He does not let me make my rounds in the wilderness!"
The trapper's father spoke to him saying:
"My son, there lives in Uruk a certain Gilgamesh.
There is no stronger than he,
he is as strong as the Meteorite of Anu.
Go, set off to Uruk,
tell Gilgamesh of this strange man.
He will give you the harlot Shamhat, take her with you.
The woman will overcome the man as if she were strong.
When the animals are drinking at the watering hole
have her take off her robe and expose her sex.
When he sees her he will draw near to her,

and the animals, who grew up in the wilderness with him will
       cease to know who he is."

He heeded his father's advice.
The trapper went to Uruk,
he made the journey, stood inside Uruk,
and declared to the mighty Gilgamesh.
       "There is a strange man who has come from the
            mountains,
       he is the mightiest in the land,
       his strength is as mighty as the Meteorite of Anu!
       He continually goes over the mountains,
       he continually plays at the watering hole with the
            animals,
       he stands opposite the watering hole.
       I was afraid, so I did not go up to him.
       He filled in the pits that I had dug,
       wrenched out my traps that I had spread,
       released from my grasp the wild animals.
       He does not let me make my rounds in the wilderness!"
Gilgamesh said to the trapper:
       "Go, trapper, bring the harlot Shamhat, with you.
       When the animals are drinking at the watering hole
       have her take off her robe and expose her sex.
       When he sees her he will draw near to her,
       and the animals, who grew up in the wilderness with
            him will cease to know who he is." ...

Noam Chomsky Knows Some Shit

Intimately familiar mouths manufacture your consent,
repeat it, repeat it over and over and over and over and over,
slicing the universe up with their tongues
into the beautiful little secrets that fill your heart
and ease your mind with compelling promises;

all is revealed for you in the cloud's branches . . . .
now its arms.

Leap Of Faith

I open up my head
for you to crawl into.
The transformation is decisive, the techniques manipulative;
we are simultaneous,
mythological,
internally coherent.
It is a solitary world,
where the Earth is covered with deep blue water,
where the body is the sky and then the body.

From silence the universe rises, detailed, ... a possession,
destructive of silence,
... all crazy in my heads.

• • •

I open my mouth
for you to speak with,
capturable,
dissolvable,
obscurable.

There is an immensity you would like to know,
but then forget.
All these different places ...,
they all sound the same, ... look the same;
I can feel your hand in my brain,
talking of believing:

> *I have grown up scattered, cast among the many victims*
> *plagiarized into being by the simple need for a lover. I have*
> *been beautiful and without rival; my jaw was once made of*
> *gold, I once had muscled arms and huge hands, I once had a*
> *thousand testicles and my throat was like a river.*

> You know the wind, of making the same mistake over
and over again until you are as seducable as I, until you can be

made impotent and killed three times, but still return to demand
dinner be on the table when you walk in that door.
I am love, and loathing.
I do not discriminate,
yet somehow your life and death still finds a way to coil itself
       around my throat,
aware of my potential immortality,
aware that I am the best part of you,
… some say the only part of you.

SHE CALLS ME A LIAR
   She calls me a liar,
   She feeds me poetry,
   She shapes both like clay
   Into great leaps of faith.
   She opens her mouth,
   "I exist only to be consumed."

Yom Kippur, 1973

My voice is like an angel's,
one convenient for rationalization,
welling from the covenant that you injected into me.

I stand condemned in your treason, but you forgive me,
pardon me for being shattered across the sky you look through to
your gods, thereby preserving me. I see that I cannot live without
your peace while you cannot live without offering it. It is as you
say …, that I have become yours.

I saw you take me when I wasn't looking,
silent with desires
fading us
into so very long ago.

So fast I run to you, crying out your names like rain against
the window.
They are like songs that crumble from my mouth.

The hand that defies you is me flowing from your lips, changing
you with repetitions that spew forth your secret names,
calling you beloved
and whispering you a sinner lady.

She is suspended in animated time,
vulnerable to the irony stinging conservatively and deeply,
a possibility grooved with poetic license.
All the way through, things coming apart with intoxication.

Suicide Bomber, 21 July 1999

Casually disfigured by the needs of others,
spoken of with heavy words,
with broken symbolism—
torture and pain bringing stillness to her poverty
left quietly sleeping in the art of children.

Indifferent to tomorrow being another day;
sprouting from the nothingness of your imagination
like the children you plagiarize,
all of them nameless with your shame,
all of them neatly folded and stored away in clean wooden boxes.

Scattered, harassed, alone,
self-defacing images blind you, the pilgrim,
to time
and to dreams made distant by those passing by
unseen,
and to those endured by others like hedonistic sins,
and undone like a blouse or a dress
and cast to the floor
in the passionate moment of vengence
dwelling in that abandoned place
deep deep in your heart
that you privately call Heaven,
and hope is more than mere fucking.

She Has Become ... Impossible

She desperately claws at the universe locked in her head,
it is not hers,
she cannot wrap herself around it,
or it around her.

A foundation of absence, death and craziness,
she struggles to forget
so that she may live.

She cannot even hear her own voice,
the one that barely speaks,
it is her silence that is suffocating.

"This is your name: Jo,"
is what is strategically placed in her mind,
she hears "crow" and knows she is becoming hopelessly linear.
"Jo," this is her new name.

She closes her eyes,
realizing that she has become utterly impossible.
She simultaneously becomes beautiful and disfigured,
she cannot breathe,
but pretends otherwise
as she always has.

The wind that is all around her does not touch her face;
The metaphors that collectively have become her eyes and ears
              and nose and skin and tongue
are no longer tethered by gravity,
no longer contained by the mere will of the gods;
again, she has become ... impossible, imprisoned.

Her body is somebody else's,
she is delicate with nonexistence,
except for her name;
her name is hers
and overflowing with perfect being.

A Death In Vain

Easing yourself off of me,
I sense you slowly disappearing into the morning mist,
enfolded in its life affirming grayness.
You whisper into me that I am unaware of this,
of you disappearing from lengthy beginning to immediate end.

Quiet dreams melt your reality-flesh away so that you
may know me in every conceivable way and through every
conceivable dimension, manifold or otherwise, although I am not
locally Euclidean.

You are peeled back so that I may taste that which I have always
        only seen.
An explosion of sensations has been your only secret fantasy,
… but I shouldn't know this,
not the way that I do, not all alone in this crowd of disciples
        that chant your name yet secretly wonder how things
        could have come to this.

You and I are the art that is somehow more than the
sound of our nihilism dropping to the ground and shattering into
a thousand sharp pieces, some of which will one day find their
eternal peace buried deeply within your skin.

I am sorry for the dreams that I have breathed into you when
        you thought that you were asleep.
I am sorry for the cuts that I have made across your face and
        hands and feet and side,
and for the punctures that do little more than confess me in
        your words.

Without so much as a cry for help, you transform into
the tempest you were certain you were destined to be, a dozen

generations of failures inciting you to commit crimes against your body that no God could hope to inspire. You become your own euphemism when you think the others have accepted your pleasure, but this shall be your undoing, as it was for me.

The Little Girl

By counting her faces you can tell how many times she has been
        stripped naked,
an arbitrary life she now wields full of great distances
and unrestrained thoughts without consequences.

She slips into the shadows so that she does not have to feel
        any more pain,
her hands open and anxious to know any heaven.

Most of the time she wishes only to be adequately preserved,
and too for someone to one day mourn her passing.

The child burned to death in her womb is the only dream or
        nightmare she allows herself to admit:
> *little girl*
> *with raven eyes*
> *and midnight hair,*
> *walking quietly now*
> *but only at night.*

Dark Matter

I am everywhere, at all times
something else altogether,
no procession of shadows struggle for the wind that speaks my
       birth syllable by syllable by syllable,
no procession of propagandists to wipe the sweat from my brow.

                Where is my life,
                insinuated,
                furious? . . . .

Crooked stained fingers,
they smell of cigarettes,
they could be a metaphor of promises not kept … but they aren't.

There is a slowness I think I remember,
and by custom, no noise;
she has a body, a woman's body,
but she is a ghost, although she doesn't believe it.

Her voice and the way she moves is mechanical, industrial;
she cannot distinguish between minutes and seconds,
but then again, she never could.

                            Some time later:
She died inward, collapsed into a black hole with virtually no
dimension; her name was Mary
and she mattered.

Dragonfly

… silent.
A memory.
Content to sell the dreams of who you wish you could be—
half-smoked abstract Rimbaudian illuminations
and a cup of cold promises you cannot keep, … black.

The world is reduced in your reflection,
alternating crowns of thorn and flower
proudly worn as if you were king
rather than a whore …
or maybe not a whore:

> *Surrounded by, … or maybe captured in,*
> *some cool and gray and dead winter.*
> *Your head turns away,*
> *your body continues straight,*
> *your face wants to run away, … very far away ….*
> *A love poem perches upon your lips*
> *without an immediate destiny,*
> *seemingly delicate … like a dragonfly.*

Silent.
A memory.
Anguished heart.
Shattered soul.
Life receives her smoothly;
she can look into anyone and say, "I am."
She knows emptiness
but will not accept it into any of her pliable bodies.
Weeping and laughing are the same to her;

"if you take a handful of clay and then smash your fist into it,
pull it, push your thumbs into it, fold the outside into the middle,
and then again, and then again, you can recreate my mind. Pour

water into a glass, swirl it quickly around and around, slosh
most of it out; you have made my body.
Almost-intransitive: I am either/or;
A great leap of faith ...
yes,
I can fly, ...
a memory,
or maybe not, not this time."
(Her words, not mine.)

Over . . . And Over . . . And Over . . .

… A thick string of redundancies obscure my heaven,
methamphetamine-god twisted all around my brain,
a mind wildly lustful, angular and irregular;

I stand before you a messiah . . . . kind of;
360 degrees without opposition—

                              jump up,
                              dress,
                              eat toast,
                              pee,
                              run far far far far far far
far far far far far far far far

                              I die, *suicide murders my body.*

Desolate watchtower, cloudless blue sky.
Infinite desert
over and over again ….

                    Clarity, exactly where I thought it would be;
                         we know the truth about you
                         a two dimensional space of mirrors.
                         Overflowing.
                         Desolate kisses are all that is left.
                              Without a mouth.
                              Smelling of rotting men that
                              used to tell you not to tell.

                         … *so cold.*

The Harlot

… The trapper went, bringing the harlot, Shamhat, with him.
They set off on the journey.
On the third day they arrived at the watering hole,
and the trapper and the harlot sat down at their posts.
A first day and a second they sat waiting.
The animals arrived and drank at the watering hole,
the wild beasts arrived and sated their thirsts with water.
Then he, Enkidu, offspring of the mountains,
who grazes with the gazelles,
came to drink at the watering hole with the animals,
with the wild beasts he sated his thirst with water.
Then Shamhat saw him—a savage,
a barbarian from the depths of the wilderness!

> "That is he, Shamhat! Release your fear,
> expose your sex so that he can take in your
> voluptuousness.
> Do not be restrained—take his energy!
> When he sees you he will draw near to you.
> Spread out your robe so he may lie upon you,
> and perform for this savage the task of womankind!
> The animals, whom he lives in wilderness with will
> become alien to him,
> and his lust will groan over you."

Shamhat released her bosom, exposed her sex, and Enkidu
took in her voluptuousness.
She was not restrained, she took his energy.
She spread out her robe and he lay upon her,
she performed for the savage the task of womanhood.
His lust groaned over her;
for six days and seven nights Enkidu stayed aroused
and had intercourse with the her
until he was sated by her charms.
But when he returned his attention to the animals,

the gazelles saw Enkidu and ran away,
the wild animals distanced themselves from him.
Enkidu raised up his depleted body,
but his knees that wanted to go off with his animals went rigid;
Enkidu was diminished, he could not run as he did before.
But then he drew himself up, for his knowledge had broadened.
Turning around, he sat down at Shamhat's feet,
gazing into her face, his ears attentive as the harlot spoke.
The harlot said to Enkidu:

>"You are beautiful, Enkidu, you are as becoming as a god.
>Why do you live in the wilderness with the wild beasts?
>Come, let me bring you into Uruk-Haven,
>to the Holy Temple, the residence of Anu and Ishtar,
>the place of Gilgamesh, who is wise to perfection,
>but who struts his power over the people like a wild
>>bull." ...

Fly Away

Redefining myself bitter and selfish and angry;
with a razor-sharp knife I carve a large chunk of you from the
      skin on my chest, over my heart, … or where my heart
      would have been had you not eaten it when we were
      children.

I close my eyes and cover my ears,
I could easily be nothing.

If I were a sword I would know exactly who I am—
an inflexible wing;
I could carve myself from your body
and fly away, … free.

I would dream myself a butterfly … or dragonfly,
and you would not recognize me.
I would be beautiful
and understand everything as it should be understood, …
unmolested.

Runaway

I think I may remember the endless crying, the shallow
       breathing when she slept.
I can imagine the emptiness again, the contradictions between
       love and occupation.
She pretended me into emptiness,
a journey of silent oblivion that she found intimately fulfilling.

She would keep her hands closed to me, repeat her heart thusly.

Without communicating, she could mean everything,
represent the universe in pure abstract terms,
do so with or without the poison of others.

She will not allow me to sink and drown, … just sink.
She is a violent storm by her own admission,
but she cannot make herself rain or lightning or thunder,
not even with the help of drugs—propagandistic or explosive.
But she is so good at pretending; after all, she pretended me so
       masterfully.

When she was a child I was her only friend, when too I was
       a child.
Nobody would believe her, … except me, I was the only
       exception,
the only one she could find in her head when she most needed
       to be believed.

She could see strangers in everyone and everything,
blend them into one
like she blends Heaven and Hell into one.
She used to be far less accomplished;

I can only lie down in the cold and die … doing so every day,
when I choose to remember her… as she remembers me.

Untitled 18

And through the nakedness of time
he resisted,
simultaneous with necessity,
resurrected without absolutes or destiny;
he never allowed his body to ever again burn,
he never allowed himself to be anything again but assumed.

A series of disfigured redundancies are what used to make him
real, but that was before.
He would often find himself... , well, ... crazy ... and absent,
crazy and absent ... and informal.
The craziness would one day become his only love, when the
emptiness had come and gone,
long after his obsession with death and the uncertainty of an
eternal heaven.

He could so easily invent his mind, fold memories into
memories and then fold those into another *ad infinitum*.

He refused to accept the amnesia, even long after it had
uttered itself so very deeply into most of (but not all of) his
consciousnesses.

He was always another language, deaf and blind to the
poetry swirling crazily around his head ... and sometimes around
his mind ... but never around his brain, the poetry that was so
easily, at least then, lifted off the ground by the wind. He was
always another language, always intuitive, never surprised. It was
all of this that made our crime so, ... well, astonishing.

I Am Icarus

I am the knife plunging, stabbing, the one that is repeated like a
       mantra, over and over and over, cutting, wandering
       disguised among the troops before the battle.
So much pain, I stand before you a mutilated man,
angel-like wings torn from my body,
wanting to fly high, …
into and beyond the sun you pray to with so much anticipated zeal,
wanting to fly higher and higher
and higher still.
      I am an Icarus: faces and more faces, … of innocence;
they will all burn. I am going insane with jealousy, insane with
the incredible heat that both murders me and sustains me.

The Little Misunderstanding

I get you all scribbled down,
you look something like this:

I tried to stay in the lines.

I just figured it out:
there is no such thing as "the real world."

I'm not sure,
but I don't think I care,
I don't think that I care that you aren't.

Britain took control of Palestine after World War I and endorsed Foreign Secretary Arthur J. Balfour's proposal of a "national home" for the Jews. The British promised to respect the rights of non-Jews in the area, and to allow Arab leaders to have their own independent states. The misunderstanding: the Arabs thought that what was meant was that Palestine was to be an independent Arab state.

Untitled 23

In my confusion you cannot commit to my silence,
you seize my face in your hands and kiss my mouth and eyes
        with well-worn words that have belonged to many others
        before stumbling upon me in your mouth.

In my mouth you become words that I cannot speak;
these pieces of me are your miracle,
a simile coiling snake-like around your throat as if it were ours,
bringing life to the voice in my head
without invalidating the child growing in you.

I smell you broken so that you may know your own self without
        induction or deduction,
so that you may know your words without asking for help.
I am merely symbolic as I weep,
carved into the past by metaphorical chisel and knife.
You have seen me this way for what seems like an eternity now,
all full of similes that do little more than predict my existence,
or perhaps a myth of far-reaching implications beyond your own
        mastery.

I am wet, but I feel myself dry when the words are beautiful.
Droning on and on, I have found my salvation in the absurd,
just as you have in me.
Hidden as I am, I am still your duty.
This foundation I am joined with in theory only tastes
        something like your sustenance,
that which was conjured from blood and semen and the dark
        fertile soil,
the story we both find so sad … and pathetic.

This is my problem: my head was copied from your head.
I dream myself the allegory stolen from the caves you and the
        others hide in,

and yet you still believe me the savior,
assumed possible for no reason other than the artist you are
    demands it so.

I have spent my lifetime, in one form or another, incinerated;
    I have spent my lifetime raped by the ineffectual love
that was invoked from the bowels of the universe to protect me
from these sinning hands of mine, these gifts, the ones you will
not admit to, not without my guiding hand.

    Does this seem impossible? But then I only seem
impossible because I am. Some day you will know what
that means. Some day you will become me in the moments
before I become nothing but an infinite number of possibilities,
possibilities you will write about with opaque imagery, and do so
pregnant, and do so with a murderous weapon.

Untitled 25

Saddled by reality and irretrievably oppressed,
he is potentially knowledge and power and wealth,
a systematic mind teetering on the precipice of fatal disaster.

It is his ecstatic control alone that gives meaning to the deepest
        truths.
He knows that oppression does not come from armies and unfair
        economic systems alone,
he knows that oppression comes from the dead,
the dead in his head.

He is a dreamer of dreams, … but who isn't.
He knows that the sound of his voice is irrelevant.
"I feel awash with absurdity,
nothing more than a transitional reference to purely cognitive
        arguments for hedonism."
This is his bizarre reality that he often talks of.
        He often cowers to his own chaos, lets it dominate him,
coerce him into thinking of himself as something other than the
original prophet.

He says it is the struggle that inspires his passion,
but I do not believe him.

"Why is it that you know?"
He says I just do, that somewhere deep down inside I just know.
"In a way different from the way you once knew there was a god?"
He says, "No, this is different."

Untitled 21

It may have been the child growing in you that you felt, you
        know it now,
now even though everyone you know has given up on you,
forgotten you,
forsaken you,
no longer recognizes you.

Words like those do not even have meaning for you even though
        you usually think they do.
When you feel like you are me, I want you to know that I have
        unraveled you, made you with suicide.
You will always be afraid here, in this bed of strangers,
always be a stranger afraid in heaven's bed.

I hear your voice next to me, shapeless, without context,
new, warm, like home. It whispers at me,
wishing only to suffocate the voice that should not speak to me.
It stands naked waiting for my name to come raining its acid
        down upon your face,
scarring you so that you cannot look beautiful in anyone's mirror
        but mine.

I have found immortality in impermanence, and impermanence
        in the dreams of a moth that I could not help but become
        before plucking its wings.
Completely devoid of contexts except those desired by some
        abstraction,
I am waiting to burn in your flame.
        • • •
Do you understand what I mean?
Do you hear me? … .
I am waiting to burn in your flame.

Untitled 20

You can no longer see me as anything but oblivion,
for those who only seek shadows are capable only of performing
    shadow plays.
The child of your naivete is my only order,
a grotesquely experimental order.
In my own mind there can be no eternity apart from my own less
    than eloquent mortalities.
There can be no more pretending, no more denial.

When the sun sinks down will they know from where they came?
Will they know who wears the crown?
I am apart from all of this, apart from the wounds that have
    come to define you.
It is the mighty one that you feel buckling under your
    cumulative weight,
a contingency motivated by the primal stirrings,
the screams in your head that are little more than your loving
    indifference.

Is this salacious freedom that you mimic crying your dissolution,
stealing your accusations with its hands?
I have tasted this betrayal on your lips before.
I remember the fever slitting the throat of my unrevealed names,
leaving them to die and rot at my sterile feet.

I appear unconvinced, round with apathy that is little more than
    my cumulative pathos.
You say that I feel like being this way, imprisoned as I am,
but I could not be so alone,
not without the pleasure of your body that you promised me
    when I was very young.

I know, you cannot accept me.
I feel you so directionless, in the pit of my stomach,
written as deeply as you are in the prayers discharged across
        your stomach in impregnating globs that smell like sour
        acquiescence.
Need I be in your head, memories, in any other way?

Navigating this sea of unrepeatable hope is that which makes
        me weary,
seized by the gilded hands of the composing and strangled until
        I give up my one secret note for them.

I am the father abdicated,
marked with proof as if I were an adulterer,
imagined the carnal pleasures that stagger about in your songs
        drunk and unruly.
Do you taste the cadence?
Can you feel it numbing your tongue with its gospel?
I have never demanded so much, not in the unfathomable depths
        of these vicious commandments that you sing of as if
        they were wholly apart from your own infractions.

Untitled 19

I dream myself awake hoping to be able to look inside and see
what you see.

The power to express what's in your mind (I cannot
see the details, not naked as I am, not when I am nothing but
somebody else's silence.) To a certain degree I am nothing but
the universals I loath so much but also know must have some
truth. Which ones are true and which are false, however, are not
up to me.

Meaning, truth? When I step into the light, I open my arms
and try to grasp all of the warmth.
I am standing here waiting,
cool to the touch, but ok.
I am grateful, although nearly dead.
Dylan Thomas writes:
Rain fades into a young death,
worn thin by pitiless acts of a distant God.
Washed away in heavy water,
stained with ink,
she swims around
and around,
unbound fates, cruel
with the gravity of the ocean
left unanswered.

This must be a translation, for I am walking in the water,
kicking the foam out of my way, my shoes in my hand, my
hair blowing in the wind. When I walk the ocean I become the
temptations I feel; I could just run in and pretend none of this
ever happened, including me, especially me. I could swim out
into the sea and never return, just keep on swimming, never
stopping,

       swim …

          forever.

Free ...

She did not know obsession, but she could see it in the mirror-eyes of the people that frequently stood directly in front of her.

There was a certain magical imagery she liked to invoke, between her determinism and her madness.

Like her madness, she was specifically located in an area of unforeseeable freedom, where frenzy is ... untethered; and like her madness, she borrowed her mask from some animality said to be written deeply in her passionate brain.

Free ... but not human.

Untitled 31

The scorching sun scribbled deeply into his face;
staring up into the face of God, "This isn't the place for memories."
He would often say such things to himself when he thought he
        might be free
and when he thought he might be alone.

In The Cup Of The Prophet's Hands

Collecting the lives of the now living … now dead,
in the cup of my hands,
making it possible for them to sleep without sedatives
or without nightmares.

It is reality that they thirst for,
reality both before and after their destiny,
before and after the cool sweetness of the flowing salvation
dispensed with the cup of one or another prophet's hands.

I heard a news report a few minutes ago about how millions of African children have been orphaned as a result of the AIDS retrovirus. The reporter said that by 2007 there will be an equivalent number of American children and African "AIDS-orphans." The reporter went on to say that unless things change quickly and dramatically most of these "AIDS-orphans" will almost certainly be left to fend for themselves on the streets.

It Takes A Village

He possesses a body, and the body a head, and the head
very
complicated
content.
Sometimes his breathing is cyclical—thorough and then
patient—
it could be thoughts (in a different life),
… but it isn't.

With a knife he writes strange love poems
into my unaccustomed heart;
The pain is …,
strange.

In my brain I am …
naked … and sometimes invisible …
and sometimes cool to the touch.
When I was young this would have been a nightmare rather than
          a dream inside my cable-t.v. head.

Way down here no one uses his name.
He no longer has arms (he is disintegrating);

his hands are compelled to silence,
forced to stare out over the sea that is the rest of eternity
without eyes.

Some of his bodies reluctantly admit to being violated—
thick heads of stone chiseled furiously until they are square
and angular, architecturally there are no smooth curves, … no
longer.

He is almost cubistic.
His body is no longer artistically interesting,
no longer … worthy of love.

"O' God, father, won't you grant me … life," he prays,
"… just this once."

To Uruk

… What she, Shamhat, said interested Enkidu.
Becoming aware of himself, Enkidu sought a friend.
Enkidu spoke to the harlot:
> "Shamhat, take me with you to the sacred Holy Temple,
>> the residence of Anu and Ishtar,
>
> the place of Gilgamesh, who is wise to perfection,
> but who struts his power over the people like a wild bull.
> I will challenge him and tame him.
> Let me shout out in Uruk: 'I am the mighty one!'
> Take me there and I will change things;
> he whose strength is mightiest is the one born in the
>> wilderness!"

Shamhat spoke to Enkidu:
> "If this is your wish, then join me,
> let us go so Gilgamesh may see your face.
> I will lead you to Gilgamesh—I know where he will be.
>
> Look about Enkidu, inside Uruk-Haven,
> where the people show off in their finest clothes,
> where every day is a day for some festival,
> where the lyre and the drum play continually,
> where harlots stand about prettily,
> exuding voluptuousness, full of laughter,
> and on the couch of night the sheets are spread.
>
> Enkidu, you who do not know how to live,
> I will show you Gilgamesh, a man of raging emotions.
> Look at him, gaze at his face—
> he is a handsome youth, with vitality,
> his whole body exudes voluptuousness.
> He has mightier strength than you,
> without sleeping day or night!

Enkidu, it is your wrong thoughts you must change!
It is Gilgamesh whom Shamash loves,
and Anu, Enlil, and Ea have expanded his mind.

Even before you came from the mountain
Gilgamesh in Uruk had dreams about you; I will tell
          you of them so that you may know the man." ...

Meditation on the Iraqi/American Attack on the Kurds

Penetrating threats of elimination
and of forgetting
stain the ground like bruises and cake my hair like dried blood
and poison the sky with macabre laughter until it turns
so dark it smells like rain
and tastes like the face of the person you will be for the rest
of your life,
the person that will repeat all the mistakes you can possibly
imagine with or without those thick words you carry
deeply carved into the Christian cross worn around
your neck.

Voices that are not my own speak to me in my mind and all
over my body,
voices which are now mine because I sleep with the mouths they
were vomited from.

If You Are My Cross

I suffer these stories into her heart.
I poured myself carefully into your body,
so very anxious with prophecy.

If you are my cross,
then this is my crucifixion.
I have stolen it from somewhere in your head,
from somewhere in the deep deep past.

Sleeper

You are a sleeper,
you dream things …
and some of those things are people.

Without your things you are anxious.
Days, months, years … you are anxious without them,
and I remind you of when you were without time,
when permanence was about eternity rather than inflicting pain,
which disturbs you … and your sleep.

You collect nights,
gather them without grieving,
create in them with a personal and private destruction
that is an impossible art for anyone else.

Eternal darkness is the blood that courses through your veins,
a holy propaganda that is your lullaby.
You can only sleep well with it echoing in your head.

Dream

They might be ghosts,
they look down into her head with eyeless faces.
The space between their thoughts is cold and lifeless
and passionately heavy.

Dreamer

Feeling you end dark in the corner, awaiting your voice
for a chance at eternity, a whispered cry of yours is my only song,
the only sound in my head. You will, one day, imitate the ocean's
roar, … and I will swim.

I breathe out for you, exhale in music the stale beauty long imprisoned in your lungs. You will seek an unrestrained silence that will be a powerful melody, and tremble poets without words into a world without language, their pulsing heartbeat a sort of hymn of ecstasy that you will steal and hide in your head.

I am the soft hand stroking your hair, easing your nightmare. But there will be another.

I can already hear you crying, the truth scalding your lips as he gently passes it into your mouth; … but now there are words.

If I could just pretend that I am the extent of the universe you sleep …, but he destroys everything I can possibly be, obliterates my absolute devotion without cause or provocation, rapes my infinite love for you with a story that is his (now maybe yours), and in his (now maybe your) language, not mine, and not in my language.

Sleep

You were once simple,
more than a broken fragment of someone else's destiny; …
suicide aside,
his words never existed in me without you,
they were merely the life that thickly flowed down from the
        song you sing in your head to help you sleep,
down and around my hands and wrists, beyond the open wounds,
to the floor
where you like to dream.

The Dreams

… Gilgamesh awakened one morning and revealed a dream,
        saying to his mother:
    "Mother, I had a dream last night.
    Stars of the sky appeared,
    and a meteorite similar to the Meteorite of Anu fell next
        to me.
    I tried to lift it but it was too heavy for me,
    I tried to turn it over but I could not budge it.
    The people of the Land of Uruk were standing around it,
    everyone from near and far had assembled about it,
    The people were thronging around it,
    the men clustered about it
    and kissed its feet as if it were a little baby.
    I loved it and embraced it as a wife.
    I laid it down at your feet,
    and you made it compete with me."
The mother of Gilgamesh, the wise, all-knowing, said to her lord;
Rimat-Ninsun, the wise, all knowing, said to Gilgamesh:
    "As for the stars of the sky that appeared
    and a meteorite similar to the one of Anu fell next to you,
    you tried to lift it but it was too heavy for you,
    you tried to turn it over but you were unable to budge it.
    The people of the Land of Uruk were standing around it,
    everyone from near and far had assembled about it,
    you laid it down at my feet
    and I made it compete with you,
    and you loved and embraced it as a wife.
    This means there will come to you a mighty man, a
        comrade who saves his friend,
    he is the mightiest in the land, he is strongest,
    his strength is as mighty as the Meteorite of Anu!
    You loved him and embraced him as a wife;
    and it is he who will repeatedly save you.
    Your dream is good and lucky!"

A second time Gilgamesh said to his mother:
> "Mother, I have had another dream:
> at the gate of my marital chamber laid an axe,
> and people had collected about it.
> The people of the Land of Uruk were standing around it,
> everyone from near and far assembled about it,
> the people were thronging around it.
> I laid it down at your feet,
> I loved it and embraced it as a wife,
> and you made it compete with me."

The mother of Gilgamesh, the wise, all-knowing, said to her son;
Rimat-Ninsun, the wise, all knowing, said to Gilgamesh:
> "The axe that you saw is a man.
> You loved him and embraced him as a wife,
> but I have made him compete wth you.
> This means there will come to you a mighty man, a
>   comrade who saves his friend,
> he is the mightiest in the land, the strongest,
> he is as mighty as the Meteorite of Anu!"

Gilgamesh spoke to his mother saying:
> "By the command of Enlil, the Great Counselor, so may
>   it be!
> May I have a friend and adviser,
> a friend and adviser may I have!
> You have interpreted for me the dreams about him!"

After the harlot recounted the dreams of Gilgamesh to Enkidu
the two of them made love. …

Four Meditations On
"Operation Iraqi Freedom"

I

PART ONE: ODE TO THOMAS KUHN

Change.
Change.
Change.
Change.
Change.

Change.
Change.

Change.

Change.

Change.

Change.
Change.
Change.

Change.
Change into anything with wings.

PART TWO

Since I have known you you have been a mouthful,
a mouthful,
a mouth full.
My mouth is full of you and what you have to say.

PART THREE

Mom really wants me to call him dad
or even daddy, …
not Paul.

PART FOUR

If I were two or three again
I wouldn't remember anything about this when I am older.

My Step Dad Loves Me is a good title for this poem—**I**.

II

Artificial Groove

Randomly assigned to this life or that,
an ironic history
pasted haphazardly across some kind of blue cardboard sky;
I venture off, trying, beyond my body,
beyond my mouth
and everything it might say.

I look in the mirror and all there is is a flat old man
pretending multidimensionality,
all there is is a strange delusion, spiritual perhaps,
that I think I fear talking about ... with these words,
these words that have
1) been in your mouth for so very long,
2) been made passionate love to and with, and
3) explained away the physical universe all over my neck and face.

And I think of a good title for a poem:
> **HAVE I SOLD MY SOUL? WOULD I KNOW IT IF I HAVE?**
... and too the first line:
> *I feel them, the ... rules, abuzz, ... in and out of my nose*
> *and mouth, I swat them away furiously; it is a*
> *peculiar dance.*

My brain feels like it is unraveling from the inside out.
I feel like I need to push my eyes in hard with my thumbs.

    I feel like I should sit down and write poetry, but it feels
like there is nothing of meaning in me anymore. It* used to push
its way into my head passively, passive-aggressively, in through
my mouth and nose. My thoughts were commissioned thusly.

---

* "It": The inspiration, a restless river pushing me down into its breast (I panic,
don't want to breathe, allow it into my lungs, but this is where I live ... my
home), a waning man dreaming his own private moon, a moon that will forever
carry his name, or one very nearly like it.

Within his head burns the last heaven.
He can bring me to my knees with only his breathing:
>   *out*
>   *in*
>   *out*
>   *in*
>   *out*
>   .
>
>   .
>
>   .

The mythology kissed into being with his last great act of sanity
is my only nurishment,
his contorted womb,
my only home.

My heart emerges violently from your chest,
a poem perfect, a moment of perfect clarity.
I am bent into awkward shapes, most I do not recognize,
but I am at peace, … strangely.

I feel you manuevering me into your mouth;
will you swallow me … or just speak with my tongue?

It is hard for me to use my eyes,
I cry your name out of my eyes,
my eyes want to be sad … and sleep without dreaming.

I need the images
of you
in my head
to be perfectly true.
My face like this is an anomaly;
and too my body, the one you enjoy so very much when I am away,
enjoy artificially
and with an artificial groove.

III

If Carver Were A Postmodern Poet He Might Have Written
Something Sort Of Like This

Scribbled in big black letters: ***PAUL,***
                            READ ME
      Unfold the paper.

Tenuously holding on.
A secret we both keep from ourselves,
struck furiously over and over and over and over and over
again.

Conditional love
bruised into my face and chest and back and arms:
permanent ink.

A ruined heart,
bruised heart,
naked heart,
crushed heart,
silent heart,
falsified heart,
attacked heart,
consumed heart,
masked heart,
… heart that now
… merely pumps blood.
      I know she is probably in our bedroom, crying, waiting
            for me to do I don't know what.
      I take a swig of beer and put the can back down on
            the table.
      I hold the paper up to my nose, it smells new.
      Her handwriting is very legible.

IV

Ode To The Man
That Raped And Impregnated
My Twelve-year-old Daughter

Her image is detached from your eyes,
her face undecipherable, perhaps Picasso-esque.
She is momentarily the oblivion you furiously paint on
        canvasses that are bellies,
she is the momentary completion you find in the defacing of an
        other's memories.

It is the illusion of victory
in your head,
the reaction to a visceral propaganda that has descended down
        upon you from some insane heaven,
that imagines this to be the map, the atlas, of your legitimate life.

When I close my eyes I see hands, I know they must be yours,
they are familiar hands.

Self Portrait 1

And my sanity, scandalized, suffering, cruel,
malicious mask, volatile mask.
And the mask cried out to me, cried out,
not pretending:
> I am little more than a self portrait
> magnificent to behold
> but unholdabe

Half crazy,
I am all abstract ...
but not just in my head
or across my face
or all across my body and memories.

Mask:
carnal, brilliant, abandoned, lonely,
obtuse face, plastic face.
And the face cried out to me,
in a child's falsetto:
"we might already be dead."

Uncertain of the symbolism that paints my lips and eyes and
cheeks,
what I remember is without passion, there was no passion.

I could just as easily be an idea, a thought, obedient, smooth.
But then I wouldn't have a different face,
maybe ugly.

I would be unrecognizable
and wholly contingent
on your belief system.

Self Portrait 2

She sleeps tangled.
She is translucent, never once opaque.
She has been abandoned,
abdicated by reality, forgotten,
left unfinished by her own God.

Now I am in this forever,
dirty with the unspeakably evil,
growing out of control like a cancer,
unimaginable screams dwelling permanently in my throat next
        to the love songs I dream of singing you in.

Self Portrait 3

*…and the doctor looks at you and says that he is sorry, but there
is nothing else he can do. He says he can control the pain, but
other than that he just doesn't know what else can be done.*

*He pulls a piece of torn paper out of the trash can and
scribbles on it. He stands up, shakes your hand and then mine.
He walks out the door, the little scrap of paper having been
transferred from his palm to mine.*

> *Matthew Black, MD*
> *La Clínica del Río Verde*
> *27 calle Río Verde*
> *Tijuana, Mexico*

Memoirs

I am an arrow,
full of symbolism....

I am bleeding,
pierced....

I am flowing,
overflowing with destiny....

I am washed in solitude,
a solitary traveler....

I am coolness,
a heart turning to ice....

I am a memory,
electrons bouncing around in sombody's head....

I am "a great man,"
"loving husband," " loving father"....

I am love carved into my hard gray face,
for loved ones....

I am sharp and steel,
unforgiving.

Like A Jackson Pollack Painting

Descending,
desolate place,
catching my reflection in a mirror.

Slow emptiness of his hand,
perfumed betrayal,
distance.

Dreamless consorts confuse their contingencies across my skin,
(my skin is like a Jackson Pollack splatter painting),
"you are the heavenly light filtering down through the trees,
you are the bright warmth piercing the fog,
you must be, you are …
god, … yes, … you are God."

    An obsession,
    wide open like an African plain,
    they come to me,
    their mouths contorted with seriousness into funny shapes,
    shapes that make me giggle.

    But I will survive their "love,"
    prevail over it with these rapier words you fill my mouth with,
    slice into and beyond the surface diseases;

I could be the gods.

Enkidu And The Harlot

... Enkidu sits in front of her, saying:
> "I have had a dream similar to Gilgamesh's.
> Stars of the sky appeared,
> and a meteorite similar to the Meteorite of Anu fell next
> > to me.
> I tried to lift it but it was too heavy for me,
> I tried to turn it over but I could not budge it.
> The animals of the wilderness were standing around it,
> every gazelle from near and far had assembled about it,
> they were all thronging around it,
> the men clustered about it
> and kissed its feet as if it were a little baby."

The harlot speaks to Enkudu, saying:
> "Your dream is similar, true.
> Rimat-Ninsun said Gilgamesh's dream was good luck,
> it must be the same for you."

Enkidu spoke, saying:
> "This may be true, but I do not wish to many times save
> > the life of a wild bull like Gilgamesh."

Shamhat the harlot spoke, saying:
> "Gilgamesh is great, there are none who are greater, but
> > he is alone.
> You do not wish to many times save the life of a wild
> > bull like Gilgamesh,
> but he will become your friend as Rimat-Ninsun saw."

Shamhat and Enkidu walked to Uruk until the sun was falling
> low in the sky.
They grew near the fire of some shepherds readying themselves
> for the night.

Shamhat pulled off her clothing,
and covered him with one piece
while she covered herself with the second.
She took hold of him as the gods do
and brought him to the place of the shepherds. ...

Three Poems About The Way It Is
As Written Deeply
Into My Living Head

I

I cannot seem to let go,
to allow myself to melt into the infinite light.
My body fades in … some,
but remains, always a shadow.

II

My body is the nurturer of the universe
within which my consciousnesses exist.

I am between two realities,
one dead,
the other powerless to be born.

III

Your mind, I put it in the palm of my hand
and when I become sleepy, between my eyes.
Your mind ascends into my body,
evolves into it, into a physical realization of body
      that is infinite and perfect;
I think of your eyes when you smile, infinite and perfect.

I have known pain, awareness, destiny.
I have opened my mouth and let the flood enter and drown my soul.
Aimless wandering, without destination, searching,
searching for life … and the living.
I have stopped asking the question,
I no longer understand it, who I am,
but your smile brings me peace
and that is all that I remember needing.

Preface To The Ceremony
On The Hill

After having razed the garden and profaned the chalices and altars, the Huns entered the monastery library on horseback and trampled the incomprehensible books and vituperated and burned them, perhaps fearful that the letters concealed blasphemies against their god, which was an iron scimitar. Palimpsests and codices were consumed, but in the heart of the fire, amid the ashes, there remained almost intact the twelfth book of the *Civitas Dei,* which relates how in Athens Plato taught that, at the centuries' end, all things will recover their previous state and he in Athens, before the same audience, will teach this same doctrine anew. The text pardoned by the flames enjoyed special veneration and those who read and reread it in that remote province came to forget that the author had only stated this doctrine in order better to refute it. A century later, Aurelian, coadjutor of Aquileia, learned that on the shores of the Danube the very recent sect of the Monotones (called also the Annulars) professed that history is a circle and that there is nothing which has not been and will not be. In the mountains, the Wheel and the Serpent had displaced the Cross. All were afraid, but all were confronted by the rumor that John Pannonia, which had distinguished himself with a treatise on the seventh attribute of God, was going to impugn such abominable heresy.

Aurelian deplored this news, particularly the latter part. He knew that in questions of theology there is no novelty without risk; then he reflected that the thesis of a circular time was too different, too astounding, for the risk to be serious. (The heresies we should fear are those which can be confused with orthodoxy.) John of Pannonia's intervention—his intrusion— pained him more. Two years before, with his verbose *De septima affectione Dei sive de aeternitrate,* he had usurped a topic in Aurelian's specialty; now, as if the problem of time belonged to him, he was going to rectify the Annulars, perhaps with

Procrustean arguments, with theriacas more fearful than the Serpent ... . That night, Aurelian turned the pages of Plutarch's ancient dialogue on the cessation of the oracles; in the twenty-ninth paragraph he read a satire against the Stoics, who defend an infinite cycle of worlds, with infinite suns, to him a favorable omen; he resolved the anticipate John of Pannonia and refute the heretics of the Wheel.

There are those who seek a woman's love in order to forget her, to think no more of her; Aurelian, in a similar fashion, wanted to surpass John of Pannonia in order to be rid of the resentment he inspired in him, not in order to harm him. Tempered by mere diligence, by fabrication of syllogisms and the invention of insults, by the *negos* and *autems* and *nequaquams*, he managed to forget the rancor. He erected vast and almost inextricable periods encumbered with parentheses, in which negligence and solecism seemed as forms of scorn. He made an instrument of cacophony. He foresaw that John would fulminate the Annulars with prophetic gravity; so as not to coincide with him, he chose mockery as his weapon. Augustine had written that Jesus is the straight path that saves us from the circular labyrinth followed by the impious; these Aurelian, laboriously trivial, compared with Ixion, with the liver of Prometheus, with Sisyphus, with the king of Thebes who saw two suns, with stuttering, with parrots, with mirrors, with echoes, with the mules of a noria and with two-horned syllogisms. (Here the heathen fables survived, relegated to the status of adornments.) Like all those possessing a library, Aurelian was aware that he was guilty of not knowing his in its entirety; this controversy enabled him to fulfill his obligations with many books which seemed to reproach him for his neglect. Thus he was able to insert a passage from Origen's work *De principiis* where it is denied that Judas Iscariot will again betray the Lord and that Paul will again witness Stephen's martyrdom in Jerusalem, and another Cicero's *Academica priora*, where the author scoffs at those who imagine that, while he converses with Lucullus, other Luculluses and Ciceros in infinite number say precisely the same thing in an infinite number of equal worlds. In addition, he wielded against the Monotones the text from Plutarch and denounced the scandalousness of an idolater's valuing the *lumen naturae* more than they did the word of God. The writing took him nine days; on the tenth, he was sent a transcript of John of Pannonia's refutation.

It was almost derisively brief; Aurelian looked at it with disdain and then with fear. The first part was a gloss on the end verses of the ninth chapter of the Epistle to the Hebrews, where it is said that Jesus was not sacrificed many times since the beginning of the world, but now, once, in the consummation of the centuries. The second part adduced the biblical precept concerning the vain repetitions of the pagans (Matthew 6:7) and the passage from the seventh book of Pliny which ponders that in the wide universe there are no two faces alike. John of Pannonia declared that neither are there two like souls and that the vilest sinner is as precious as the blood Jesus shed for him. One man's act (he affirmed) is worth more than the nine concentric heavens and imagining that his act can be lost and return again is a pompous frivolity. Time does not remake what we lose; eternity saves it for heaven and also for hell. The treatise was limpid, universal; it seemed not to have been written by a concrete person, but by any man or, perhaps, by all men.

Aurelian felt an almost physical humiliation. He thought of destroying or reforming his work; then, with resentful integrity, he sent it to Rome without modifying a letter. Months later, when the council of Pergamum convened, the theologian entrusted with impugning the Monotones' errors was (predictably) John of Pannonia; his learned and measured refutation was sufficient to have Euphorbus the heresiarch condemned to the stake. "This has happened and will happen again," said Euphorbus. "You are not lighting a pyre, you are lighting a labyrinth of flames. If all the fires I have been were gathered together here they would not fit on earth and the angels would be blinded. I have said this many times." Then he cried out, because the flames had reached him.

The Wheel fell before the cross[1], but Aureliand and John of Pannonia continued their secret battle. Both served in the same army, coveted the same guerdon, warred against the same Enemy, but Aurelian did not write a word which secretly did not strive to surpass John. Their duel was an invisible one; if the copious indicies do not deceive me, the name of the other does not figure once in the many volumes by Aurelian preserved in Migne's *Patrology*. (Of John's works only twenty words have survived.) Both condemned the anathemas of the second council of Constantinople; both persecuted the Arriansists, who denied the eternal generation of the Son; both testified to the othodoxy of Cosmas' *Topographia chrisiana*, which teaches that the earth is quadrangular, like the Hebrew tabernacle. Unfortunately, to the four corners of the earth another tempestuous heresy spread. Originating in Egypt or in Asia (for the testimonies differ and Bousset will not admit Harnack's reasoning), it infested the eastern provinces and erected sanctuaries in Macedonia, in Carthage and in Treves. It seemed to be everywhere; it was said that in the diocese of Britannia the crucifixes had been inverted and that in Caesarea the image of the Lord had been replaced by a mirror. The mirror and the obolus were the new schismatics' emblems.

History knows them by many names (Speculars, Abysmals, Cainites), but the most common of all is Historiones, a name Aurelian gave them and which they insolently adopted. In Frigia they were called Simulacra, and also in Dardania. John of Damascus called them forms; it is well to note that the passage has been rejected by Erfjord. There is no heresiologist who does not relate with stupor their wild customs. Many Histriones professed asceticism; some mutilated themselves, as did Origen; others lived underground in the sewers; others tore out their eyes; others (the Nabucodonosors of Nitria) "grazed like oxen and their hair grew like an eagle's." They often went from mortification and severity to crime; some communities tolerated thievery;

[1]In the Runic crosses the two contrary emblems coexist entwined.

others homicide; others, sodomy, incest and bestiality. All were blasphemous, they cursed not only the Christian God but also the arcane divinities of their own pantheon. They contrived sacred books whose disappearance is lamented by scholars. In the year 1658, Sir Thomas Browne wrote: "Time has annihilated the ambitious Histrionic gospels, not the Insults with which their Impiety was fustigated": Erfjord has suggested that these "insults" (preserved in a Greek codex) are the lost gospels. This is incomprehensible if we do no know the Histriones' cosmology.

In the hermetic books it is written that what is down below is equal to what is on high, and what is on high is equal to what is down below; in *Zohar*, that the higher world is a reflection of the lower. The Histriones founded their doctrine on a perversion of this idea. They invoked Matthew 6:12 ("and forgive us our debts, as we forgive our debtors") and 11:12 ("the kingdom of heaven suffereth violence") to demonstrate that the earth influences heaven, and I Corinthians 13:12 ("for now we see through a glass, darkly") to demonstrate that everything we see is false. Perhaps contaminated by the Monotones, they imagined that all men are two men and that the real one is the other, the one in heaven. They also imagined that our acts project an inverted reflection, in such a way that if we are awake, the other sleeps, if we fornicate, the other is chaste, if we steal, the other is generous. When we die, we shall join this other and be him. (Some echo of these doctrines persisted in Leon Bloy.) Other Histriones reasoned that the world would end when the number of its possibilities was exhausted; since there can be no repetitions, the righteous should eliminate (commit) the most infamous acts, so that these will not soil the future and will hasten the coming of the kingdom of Jesus. This article was negated by other sects, who held that the history of the world should be fulfilled in every man. Most, like Pythagoras, will have to transmigrate through many bodies before attaining the liberation; some, the Proteans, "in the period of one lifetime are lions, dragons, boars, water and a tree." Demosthenes tells how the initiates into Orphic mysteries were submitted to purification with mud; the Proteans, analogously, sought purification through evil. They knew, as did Carpocrates, that no one will be released from prison until he has paid the last obolous (Luke 12:59) and used to deceive penitents with this other verse: "I am come that they might have life, and that they might have it more abundantly" (John 10:10). They also said that not to be evil is a satanic arrogance .... Many and divergent mythologies were devised by the Histriones; some preached asceticism, others licentiousness. All preached confusion. Theopompus, a Histrione of Berenice, denied all fables; he said that every man is an organ put forth by the divinity in order to perceive the world.

The heretics of Aurelian's diocese were of those who affirmed that time does not tolerate repetitions, not of those who affirmed that every act is reflected in heaven. This circumstance was strange; in a report to the authorities in Rome, Aurelian mentioned it. The prelate who was to receive the report was the empress' confessor; everyone knew that this demanding post kept him from the intimate delights of speculative theology. His secretary—a former collaborator of John Pannonia, now hostile to him—enjoyed fame as a punctual inquisitor of heterodoxies; Aurelian added an exposition of the Histrionic heresy, just as it was found in the conventicles of Genua and of Aquileia. He composed a few paragraphs; when he tried to write the atrocious thesis that there are no two moments alike, his pen halted. He could not find the necessary formula; the admonitions of this new doctrine ("Do you want to see what human eyes have never seen? Look at the moon. Do you want to hear what ears have never heard? Listen to the bird's cry. Do you want to touch what hands have never touched? Touch the earth. Verily I say that God is about to create the world.") were much too affected and metaphorical to be transcribed. Suddenly, a sentence of twenty words came to his mind. He wrote it down joyfully; immediately afterwards, he was troubled by the suspicion that it was the work of another. The following day, he remembered that he had read it many years before in the *Adversus annlares* composed by John of Pannonia. He verified the quotation; there it was. He was tormented by incertitude. If he changed or suppressed those words he would weaken the expression; if he loft them he would be plagiarizing a man he abhorred; if he indicted their source, he would be denouncing him. He implored divine assistance. Towards the beginning of the second twilight, his guardian angel dictated to him an intermediate solution. Aurelian kept the words, but preceded them with this notice: "What the heresiarchs now bark in the confusion of the faith was said our realm by a most learned man, with more frivolity than guilt." Then the dreaded, hoped for, inevitable thing happened. Aurelian had to declare who the man was; John of Pannonia was accused of professing heretical opinions.

Four months later, a blacksmith of Aventinus, deluded by the Histriones' deceptions, placed a huge iron sphere on the shoulders of his small son, so that his double might fly. The boy died; the horror engendered by this crime obliged John's judges to assume an unexceptionable severity. He would not retract; he repeated that if he negated his proposition he would fall into the pestilential heresy of the Monotones. He did not understand (did not want to understand) that to speak of the Monotones was to speak of the already forgotten. With somewhat senile insistences, he abundantly gave forth with the most brilliant periods of is former polemics; the judges did not even hear what had once enraptured them. Instead of trying to cleanse himself of the slightest blemish of Histrionism, he strove to demonstrate that the proposition of which he was accused was rigorously orthodox. He argued with the men on whose judgement his fate depended and committed the extreme ineptitude of doing so with wit and irony. On the 26th of October, after a discussion lasting three days and three nights, he was sentenced to die at the stake.

Aurelian witnessed the execution, for refusing to do so meant confessing his own guilt. The place for the cer …
HOLD IT. THIS IS BORGES, … JORGE LUIS BORGES.

Shit! This is Borges ... goddamnit!
I didn't write it...,

I mean, ... I wrote it ..., but I didn't write it. It was just in my head.

Goddamnit, who put that there when I wasn't looking.

... or perhaps this is an inhereted memory....
Could this be an inhereted memory?

Oh well.

Legend & Maker

In my eyes you see
your sustenance, you see
your hunger.
It is beautiful to behold,
intensely public, your dream of being ... you,
but when I look in a mirror
in my eyes you see that I see
my distractions, I see
my dream of being ... you.

[later in the day he writes ...]

It is a desolate space, ... slow, ...eyeless, vast ...
and silent. Things are often transparent here,
ghost-bodies uncertain of their existence,
even of whether or not they remember accurately
or are capable of being remembered . . . .*

*Earlier today I was wandering through the stacks at the library and I accidently stumbled onto an obscure little anthropology journal. It had a pretty neat cover so I opened it up and quickly thumbed through the pages. On the first page, which happened to be the last page since I had riffled through the journal back to front, was the conclusion of an article about traditional dances of "lost" Amazonian tribes; that is, indigenous people of the Amazon Basin that have only recently made contact with the "modern" world.

I was particularly fascinated by one of the dances performed by the "Quiet River People" of the north. Apparently, when a baby is born into them the whole tribe dances its history so that the infant will know who he or she is. The event takes place over several days and culminates with a dance performed by exactly thirty-nine of the tribes best warriors and which tells of the day their greatest warrior, Ktotl, was slain in battle and of his moment before God. God, so the story goes, looks deeply into the eyes of the vanquished warrior, and in a sudden flash of comprehension Ktotl begins to cry uncontrollably "like a baby." He will cry for eternity the legend goes, for virtually everything he had believed was, in fact, wrong.

After reading that I began to tremble, I could no longer hold the journal and it fell to the floor in a crash. Fear raced up and down my body ... uncontrollably. Tears welled up in my eyes and I somehow knew that something very profound had accidently stumbled into me. Now, hours later, I am still not completely sure what that something was, all I know is that all I want to do is spend most of my time painting, writing poetry, playing with my dog, and loving my wife and our daughters.

[he writes this next part some time later]

If I could write about it, this is what I would write ...
or something like it:
He believes himself to be young, to be between me and a
    memory of him,
lifting his face high above his head in triumph,
his nakedness deep in his pockets.

The dark inconsistencies of his life shakes its fist at him, twisted
    and lonely,
shaking him into abstract effigy that he does not fully comprehend,
a simple pleasure standing alone, blind and burned with
    another's peace.

Scattered across the desert
in deep reds and rich browns,
he has always stood abandoned

as if he were sand, the scorching sun scribbled into his face;
staring up into the face of his gods … "thank you for my life,"
he would often say aloud, but quietly,
when he thought it might make a difference.

But now he knows, knows that this place is the end of the world,
the place of marriage between thunder and lightning,
and that only a warrior's own voice can speak of it,
whisper that place in his head
where the waves roll and then come crashing down upon his
        sleeping sand body.

[he was pleased with his words so he stopped writing for the day]

Untitled 6

He could not resist the compulsion to taste his own heart,
could not pretend himself anything but a cannibal;

drunk old man, ...
drunk old man with a long gray beard.
When you are done, ...
when you are done you will simply starve to death,

your isolation preserved.

Violent Homeland

Violent homeland,
a shapeless body,
wholly recognizable;

a perfect representation
sculpted in murder and convenient forgetting.

Addict-Mouth

You kiss me onto the flesh of others so you can survive for at least one moment more. You say you are kissing me but I am not so sure.

I am suffering at the hands of a total stranger,
jealous with delusions both sharp and cool;
through nights like this one I once held her in my arms,
my soul is not satisfied that it has lost her.
The echoes of her sweet poetry-voice try to form the shape of
       my own mouth;
I found it on the floor
convulsing
curled up, hiding, in the shadows ... my addict-mouth.

Crawling in next to your body late at night, I scream myself into what remains secretly incestuous, what remains coveted by broken men slashed across your wrists with memories only Heaven can remove.

She is a wind swept place
without sun, stars or moon,
a dark asylum she pretends not to inhabit.
She is stained with,
scarred by, entangled in,
a completely obscuring sanity haphazardly cut onto her body
and into her head.

With The Shepherds

… The Shepherds gathered all around about Enkidu,
they marveled:
>"How the youth resembles Gilgamesh—
>tall in stature, towering up to the battlements over the wall!
>Surely he was born in the mountains;
>his strength is as mighty as the Meterorite of Anu!"

The shepherds placed food in front of Enkidu,
they placed beer in front of him.
Enkidu knew nothing about eating bread for food,
and of drinking beer he had not been taught.
The harlot spoke to Enkidu, saying:
>"Eat the food Enkidu, it is the way one lives.
>Drink the beer, as it is the custom of our land."

Enkidu ate the food until he was sated,
he drank the beer—seven jugs!—and became expansive and
>sang with joy.

He was elated and his face glowed.
He splashed his shaggy body with water,
and Shamhat rubbed him with oil, turning him into a human.
He put on some clothing and became a warrior.
He routed the wolves, and chased off the lions,
with Enkidu as their guard the shepherds could lie down and rest.
In the next daylight Enkidu rested.

At high sun the two left the shepherds.
Enkidu spoke to the harlot, saying:
>"Why is it that Gilgamesh is a Wild Bull?
>Why is it that he is king if his people wish him to be tame?"
>"Gilgamesh does not leave a son to his father,
>day and night he arrogantly tests every man and boy to
>>prove his own greatness.
>In Gilgamensh the shepherd of Uruk-Haven,

there is no peace, he is the shepherd trusted but feared,
bold, eminent, knowing, wise,
two-thirds god, one third man, he is alone.
Gilgamesh does not leave a girl to her betrothed!"
Enkidu spoke, saying:
"Gilgamesh is king and exerts his every will upon his
people.
He needs to test his greatness against those he knows
are lesser.
Gilgamesh is said to be wise,
but I do not see wisdom.
I understand the loneliness Gilgamesh does,
for he has no equal, but there is nothing to be found in
defeating the weak.
Gilgamesh cannot find a friend by stealing the heart
of others.
Enkidu's face flushed with anger.
Enkidu's heart was full of rage.
Enkidu spoke to Shamhat, saying:
"I will teach this thief in king's robes,
I will teach him what it is to be defeated by one greater."
Enkidu walked quickly in front, and Shamhat after him. ...

Inherited Memories

My fingers and toes turn black with your mythology,
light of your day removing me from the light of another's night.
I like to think that I am no longer blind,
but everyone knows that without any effort I become the dark.

Untitled 32

The convoluted visions of illusion promise him a path of tender
      tears tearing violently at the edges of this stranger's reality.
Under these tortured skies rise the dispassionate decisions of
      place and time broken under the weight of the artist's
      brush.
Begged questions find release in this transparent fog of
      remembering, that inaccessible corridor of all that is
      virgin and wild.

Shooting stars with new and improved faces murder him,
      they are murky and sloppy and bare a withered breast as
      if they were a mother instead of a virgin whore.

Through jaded eyes you perceive both compassion and
      righteousness,
happy to define the confusion in the momentary lapses of mind,
this simple mind of mine that I only wish you could drink from.
You could take this chalice into your hands, surrender to its kiss
      and the curves of its hopelessly fouled mouth.
You could drink from it,
bring her into you.
Bring her into you and then wipe her from your lips with the
      back of your hand.
She is no longer a mystery,
no longer just blood said to be wine.

"Only God Can Save Her From God"

Her mouth has no history of openness,
but it invents words to never speak.

When it does speak all it says is
"only God can save her from God."

> And by "her" it means the woman with the mouth
> that has no history of openness.

My Body is Sadness

Where eternity is vindicated she will proclaim the pain she bears as a martyr, an abyss; like fire she has no sanctuary that she does not destroy. But she knows this, and this is what I love most about her. I love most that she can be everything that I know.

Sometimes I think you want me to destroy you.

"I hate you for this," I can hear you whisper when you think that I am asleep. I erase you.

I take my face off and invite everyone to see you:

... these are my suicide songs,
the ones you smile
with your face in your hand.

She fears she will be remembered.

With a single note you can destroy my whole life. It is what you know you believe, an incestuous desire for one of many nameless worlds, so much hunger.

She is simple, a broken fragment from my own destiny; ... suicide aside, these words have never existed in me. They are water that rolls to and beyond this little song you sing in your head to help you sleep, down and around my hands and wrists;
down and around
my hands and wrists

By chance you found that sometimes you need to rest from not being insane and not being dead ....
We both know suicide,
these hands we have become burn of it.

The gift of the impossible turns quietly toward silence,
a little memory wrapped in a familiar pain.
I have become unknown except for whom I seem to portray
      myself to be:

My body is sadness.

     MY BODY IS SADNESS
     I think I may not be God;
     I think I may be a mask,
     hiding your heroinelike body
     from the addicts suffering you in you.
              My body is sadness,
              deep, deep sadness.

     I am perfect, I know heaven, am lifted up into the
sky; I am the sacrifice, the one offered up without thinking.
I am the one that is borrowed and never returned, the blood
that you let trickle through your fingers so that its sand
becomes your time.
     I am sacrifice, but abdication is my destiny, nothing and
everything eternal, nothing and eternal my autobiography, the
one people in the distant future will read about in history books,
… where I will be without a face, where I will just be a monster
with the untellable story of an angel.

The Hand You Strike With Is Only A Fist

The assault
upon my body
was clean
and fair,
measured and self aware,
a gentle kiss made permanent without mythology
or visible love.

My will to survive,
to power,
was more than symbolic,
was more than the gesture left naked all over her face.

A peaceful dilemma was what she would later call my mind,
exalted and all alone,
... a puppet for the children in my body to play with.
I can feel my chest being torn open, my heart being ripped away
        and offered to heaven,
I can feel all of this on your lips,
the ones you pretend so very well with
when you don't think anyone is watching.

To be nurtured, embellished, ... ceremonial with ability,
to be a word that will one day later be used to kill,
this is my destiny, ...
my favorite revenge,

and do not disbelieve me as you say you must now,
for I do not know how to exist any other way.

Invisible lover, I need to be replenished by your ...
invisible love;
the hand you strike with is only a fist.

Defeat

Words cannot find my mouth, don't want to;
I am mute
and suicidal.

Oppressive acts of sanctuary
swallow me incomplete,
asking for a forgiveness untouched by the sweet sweet aria
      descending without voice
into you—

I hold her hand tightly over my mouth,
a secret hungering for peace
and to be washed in water uncontaminated with the fecal
      tongues of dark strangers rolling around in your mouth,
displacing the long series of visions that could become poems
      if they were not fundamentally cowards,
and if they would only admit their predestined defeat.

Introduction to The Upādhi

When he approaches you empty I am terrified for you, knowing
what he has done to you before. Do not think for even
one moment that I do not remember the things you used to
say in your sleep; I committed your stories to memory so
that I would not forget;
they became dessert.

He says that sometimes he feels that he was born and raised
something else all together.
Sometimes he knows that he is a mask that other people wear,
carved out of wood and ornately painted.
When it is very quiet and very dark he can feel himself on other
            people's faces,
his name on other people's lips.
He says he can feel the condensation of their breath building up
            underneath him, where he is not painted and his skin is
            not rubbed and sanded smooth.

When he is worn, he can feel the heat of what they are hiding,
their lies to others and themselves.
He feels like he is always in this premeditated state of being,
incapable of escaping the power of mouths and eyes and noses
            he covers.
He is susceptible to exploitation,
a mystic woven into the smiles he conceals.
He knows their real names, the ones no one is supposed to know,
and yet still everything he feels of them is a secret.

He leads a superficial existence,
I have seen him leading it for what seems to be my whole life.
I know him no other way,
he is who he is, scared, sad,
incapable of hiding his own emotions when no one else is around.

I feel his pain, I share his sense of the sublime.

     I know what it is like to have the universe hide behind you, using you as a shield to defend itself against the sadistic revelations that make you every bit as real as I hope that I am.

When he sleeps he knows exactly what I am thinking;
I cannot dream, not all the time; … he knows that too.
I spend my time asleep and awake.
None of it seems to make any sense to his head any more.
He knows that only he can have such profound hallucinations
        for me.
I know what it is like to be called his name, know what it is like
        to walk in the presence of an irrelevant God.
So much chaos wrapped around my head.
I too know what it feels like to be different all together,
ashamed of the tyranny he hides in his pleasure.

He knows himself hypnotic
when the mask he is is on another's face,
full of death that is not quite …
love
and not quite apathy.

Compassion is the emulsion that validates my fate, just as it
        does yours.
Illusion is so funny that way, unencumbered by the natural
        sympathies of our shared misprisonment.
I have been forsaken, but I can still feel you inside me,
organic by will and decree.
My jailer is his jailer,
mimicked naked,
the sun shining on your body,
provocatively creating and destroying you warm.

Melt into my head, your head articulated with color.

He says he cannot be sure, not with the strange humility
that has become his center of aggression. I am the culmination of
your fragmentation, a tangle of fractures and spaces kissed into a
death that no longer makes any sense to me.

You whisper in my ear that you are a butterfly, adorned
with the incestuous confessions of fathers and lovers that extol,
pacify, and atrophy you into self-reflexive redemption …
but I don't know what that means.

In my throat I can feel the tension between my stomach and mind
(it is very Shakespearean),
I find it hard to swallow, equally difficult to vomit;
the word assassin keeps echoing in my head
(in somebody else's voice),
"assassin," and too "orange"
(but "orange" is in one of my voices).

I am confused and anxious with … conflict,
inconsolable,
frozen in the enactment of a timeless mythological event that
        is both familiar and foreign.
On the one hand there are *The Angels* (Rainer Maria Rilke)—
All of them have weary mouths
and bright souls without seam.
And a yearning (as toward sin)
goes sometimes through their dream.

Almost they are all alike;
in God's gardens they keep silent,
like many, many intervals
in his might and melody.

Only when they spread their wings
are they the wakers of a wind:

As though God went with his wide
sculptor-hands through the pages
in the dark book of his first beginning.—
And on the other hand *The Assassins* (Robert Jordan Smith)—
All of them have weary mouths
and bright souls without seam.
And a yearning (as toward sin)
goes sometimes through their dream.

Almost they are all alike;
in God's gardens they keep silent,
like many, many intervals
in his might and melody.

Only when they spread their wings
are they the wakers of a wind:
As though God went with his wide
sculptor-hands through the pages
in the dark book of his first beginning.
          Rainer Maria Rilke (The Angels).

Angels on one hand, assassins on the other,
the universe uneasily cupped in the hands of a man beaten down
and beaten down into death.
I can see that your lips aren't moving,
but I can hear you asking yourself why.
I can feel the place in my heart that is damaged—
where I love you.

My life is defined by pent-up frustration;
I am obsessed with the limits of my mind and of my body,
and ... and with Picasso.
          Sometimes I think he is in my head, Picasso,
          that Picasso is in my head,
          putting both of my eyes on only one side of my face;
          it is so often so hard for me to see.

The Man Whose Elegy is His Life

He never shares his multi-colored wounds,
the too proud man,
blistered to the depths of his soul by a burning journey
some have called his life.

His mind extends from border to border,
his dying homeland a complex version of his self-declared sanity.

He is aware that there is a stranger in his body,
but refuses to admit hearing its baritone voice
or to be moved by its declarations of love
and other less subtle affections.

He highly recommends molestation.

He highly recommends molestation,
but not of his own children.
He highly recommends the molestation of other people's children.

Cyan and yellow and magenta and black justifications become
        lavender poems in his head ...
and then purple songs ...
and then chartreuse love songs ...
and then burnt umber prayers that he forgets how to repeat
but still feels compelled to mumble into alternative rainbows ...
whenever he remembers.

Things Stay The Same

And though you hide your eyes behind barbed wire,
and cover your face with the darkest shadows,
it is solitude that you fear most ferociously,
it is emptiness that you dread most wildly.

No one opens their arms wide enough for you to enter.
No one quite remembers how to smooth away the violence of
      your broken soul.
No one quite remembers how to raise you up through the storm
      into the quiet.

Your wings are so easily plucked.
Cruel children . . . turn you into them,
desolate, a desert, gray.

She wears so many years of sadness on her face and body,
your mother;
your mother calls for you to come in now,
it is getting dark and supper is almost ready,

but you and the beautiful girl with long black hair next to you
are already dead.

Dictator

His eyes were blameless, he smiled coldly,
his grip was firm and his mouth...,
his mouth was capable of execution.

He only used metaphors when there was no clearer alternative,
and his voice reminded me of the days when I was in the womb.

I recognized him without ever knowing he existed,
he knew this and played me well.
I tried to be patient and at peace.
His expectations squeezed my brain into juice.
I was his only nourishment, my Buddha mind.

He practiced redundency as if it were a religion
(he would cringe at my simile),
and he especially enjoys all of the pertinent logical fallacies.

He loves the sound of crashing ocean waves,
and the smell of ripe wild strawberries.
He has very good personal hygene... .

To this, his bodiless house, he prays,
endless and full of a curious blame.
Hands move delicately over his body,
his corpse.

He is quiet
and remembers the Rilke poem about washing the corpse.

Open Letter to Palestine

It is rare when someone else says exactly what I want to say, and even rarer when someone does so before I even know I want to say it, but that just happened.

This is from a letter allegedly written by a woman to a man serving with the North's army during the American Civil War. The man had been horribly disfigured during battle, including, I think, having both arms amputated. Upon recovering, the man wrote the woman, telling her to no longer wait for his return, that she should forget all about him and marry someone else, someone less hideous looking and more physically complete than he.

I want to share her reply with you as if her words were my own. I know that it is often difficult to love and feel me loving you during these long periods of depression and incompleteness. I know it is hard but you have to trust that I do love you, and do so with every fiber of my body, mind and soul.

Her reply:
"As long as you have a body capable of holding your soul, I will cling to it."

Eating The Unborn

"BECAUSE WE CAN" ISN'T AN ARGUMENT

My eyes have become aware without opinion,
I was born to be this standing prophecy
of a divine deliverer.

A divine man was prayed for,
expected, anticipated,
a man I could not be without assistance.

I survive in the heart of the desert,
I am a precious drop of water,
I think I am small in number…

and then you existed, you didn't and then you did.

PART II

No one inside him,
behind his face and his other face,
no one in his stormy, fantastic, copious words,
only a bit of coldness,
"only a bit of coldness," he would write. … He wrote:

**SHE KNOWS EMPTINESS,
BUT SHE DOES NOT KNOW THAT SHE KNOWS IT**

Where are you going
brown girl with a white-man's name?

124

I have no reason,
no reality,
no razor tongue for your mouth.
Bitter tasting girl,
no eyes to see herself.

She casually destroys her face with long beautiful fingernails she meticulously keeps. She knows emptiness, but does not know that she knows it.

If she could walk on the moon she might know peace, might know quiet. She might grow into this desolate space, even understand her death to be a desert.

She might leave behind secrets of violence, and love terminal. Nowhere, though, will she know herself,
no, not really.

On the palms of her hands she uses a marking pen and writes, "this is how I know my life: I am on fire, an eternity of searing heat, ... as if I where Hell." She probably does this so she will not forget.

BLACK-TIME CHILD

Went to find you,
without loneliness or struggle,
slumbering powers tangled up in oceans of disunity that
        lament the old ways ... without saying as much.
You undress, fragrant with life yet unborn,
uncertain name,
uncertain echo.
Ready to burn ... and amuse.
I've heard this meditation of excuses so many times before,
it was once strong, stronger than even I.

Burning sun rises high and fast to my east,
your nurturing propaganda warming my transparent skin,

measuring.
I feel timid ... with memories of you,
half born,
resurrected into a red sky,
. . . a warning; I am here only to warn you,
I will not bite or eat you.
The source of all of your substance talks me out of fighting
        and making you bleed;
pure body.
Ember and ice, I slip away, a forgotten essence
that is no longer pretendable,
split apart, without recognizable boundaries for you to exploit.

A statue struck blind, no more absolutes;
a cave ..., torn apart ..., resurrected ..., disappeared ....

Nothing else wants to be said except,
"In between, I have had and been so many beautiful faces."

SCHIZOPHRENIC VOICES imprison my mouth,
sell my words to saviors
resplendent with a universe of colorful drugs.
I find them lying on the floor,
convulsing an eternity of emptiness
through the dark asylum of my head, ...
waiting to murder again.

**SELECTED BIBLIOGRAPHY
IN MY RADIOACTIVE HEAD**

Aquinas, St. Thomas: *Summa Theologica*
Aristotle: *The Metaphysics*
___ *De Anima*

___ *The Nicomachean Ethics*
___ *The Politics*
___ *The Poetics*
___ *Treatise on* Rhetoric
Augustine, Saint: *City of God*
Aurelius, Marcus: *Meditations*
*Sir Fr*ancis Bacon: Novum *Organum; Essays*
*Bakunin, Mikhail: The B*asic Bakunin: Writi*ngs 1869-1871*
*Bentham, Jeremy: The Princ*iples of M*orals and Legislation*
Berkley, George*:* Three Dialogues Between H*ylas & Philonous*
*Calv*in: I*nstitutions of* the Chr*istian Religion*
*Ci*cero, *Marcus Tullius: The* Nature of the Gods
___ *On Divination*
*Darwin: The Desc*ent of Ma*n*
___ *The Origin* of *Species*
*Desc*artes, Rene: *Discourse on Method* and *The Meditations*
___ *Medit*ations *on First Philosophy*
Dewey, John: Freedom and *Culture*
___ *Individualism Old and N*ew
___ L*iberalism and Social Action*
*D*urkheim, Emi*le: Ethics* and the Sociology o*f Morals*
Einstein: G*e*neral Theory of *Relativity*
Fara*day, Michael*: T*he Forces of Nature*
*Feu*erbac*h, Ludwig: The Essence of Chr*istiani*ty*
*Freud: A Gen*eral Introd*uction to Psychoanalysis*
___ The *Interpretation of Dreams*
___ *Totem and Taboo*
*G*alileo: Discourse *on Two New Sciences*
___ Dialog*ue Concerning the T*wo Chief Worl*d System*s
Hegel, G. W. F.*: The Phi*losophy *of Hist*ory
___ *Phi*losophy of Rig*ht*
Herodotus: History
Hobbes*, Thomas: Leviathan*
Homer: Odyssey
___ *I*lliad

Hume, David: *Treatise of Human* Nature
___ *An E*nquiry Concerning *Human Understanding*
*James, William: T*he Mea*ning of Truth*
___ *Prag*matism
Kant, Immanuel: Groundwork of the M*etaphysic of Morals*
___ *Critique of Pure Reason*
___ *Critique of Practical Reason*
Keynes: General *Theory o*f Employment, In*terest, and Money*
___ *A Tract on Monetar*y Reform
Newton, Isaac: Princ*ipia*
*Leuret, Michel: Capitalism and the Illus*ion of Democra*c*y
*Liebniz, Gottfried Wilhelm: Dis*course *on Metaphysics and the*
　　　 Monadology
*Loc*ke, J*ohn: Second Treatise on Civil G*overnment
___ *An Essay Concerning* Human Understandi*ng*
___ *A Letter Con*cerning Tolera*tion*
*Lucre*tius: On The *Nature of Things*
Luther, Mart*in: On Christian Liberty*
Machia*velli: The Prince*
*Marx, K*arl: The Communist Ma*nifesto*
___ *The Poverty of Philosophy*
___ *The*ories *of* Su*rplu*s Value
Mill, John Stuart*: Considerations on Repr*esenta*tive Gove*rnment
___ On Liber*ty*
___ *Utilitarianis*m
___ Three Essays on *Religion*
___ *On Soc*ialism
*Newton, Sir I*saac: *Principia Mathematica*
Nietzsche, Fried*rich: Beyond Good* and E*vil*
___ *The* Antichri*st*
___ Thus *Spake* Zara*thustra*
Pai*ne*, Thomas: *The Age of Rea*so*n*
___ *Rights of M*an
Plato: *Apology*
___ *Crito*

____ *The Republic*
____ *Phaedo*
____ *Lysis*
____ *Phaedrus*
____ *Symposium*
____ *Protagoras*
____ *Philebus*
____ *Gorgias*
____ Laws
Rousseau: T*he Social Contrac*t
____ *On th*e Orig*in of Inequ*ality
____ A *Discourse on Po*litic*al Economy*
*Santa*yana, George: *The Life of Reason*
Sextus Empiricus: *Outlines of Pyrrhonis*m
Veblen, Thorstein: *Theory of the Leisure Class*

The Contents

The Contest

… Enkidu walked down the street of Uruk-Haven,
bold, mighty, fearless.
He blocked the way through Uruk-Haven.
The people of Uruk stood around him,
people from near and far assembled about him,
the people were thronging around him,
the men were clustered about him,
and kissed his feet as if he were a little baby.

Suddenly a handsome young man appeared in the street.
For Ishra the marital bed was ready,
Gilgamesh was to come together with the girl that night.
Enkidu blocked the marital chamber,
not allowing Gilgamesh entry.
They grappled with each other at the entrance to the chamber,
in the streets they attacked each other, in the public square of
        the land,
the doors of the houses trembled and the walls shook,

Dirt from the streets rose up into the air
Choking the throngs of people of Uruk.
Gilgamesh waged his might against Enkidu,
Enkidu waged his might against Gilgamesh,
a victor was not assured.

The two great warriors exchanged blows throughout the night
and through the next day.

Enkidu nearly the victor could not fully contain Gilgamesh's
        strength
Gilgamesh nearly the victor could not fully contain Enkidu's
        strength.

The people of Uruk grew tired, but could not leave,
their king in danger,
their liberator on the brink of defeat.

Gilgamesh and Enkidu exchanged blows in the streets and atop
        the walls.
It was a great battle,
none before had been this tightly waged.
None greater than Enkidu had ever been challenged,
none that could in the moment of a single mistake rout Gilgamesh.

None greater than Gilgamesh had ever encountered in the wild,
None that could in the moment of a single mistake rout Enkidu.

On the third day, the two great warriors continued to fight,
neither would submit,
hunger and thirst were never accepted.
The doors and walls of the houses continued to shake,
the people became tired,
begged the two to let them rest.

The ears of Enkidu and Gilgamesh were not deaf,
they heard the pleas of the people of Uruk-Haven.
Gilgamesh spoke to Enkidu, saying:
        "You Enkidu, and I have many days left in us,
        these people are already tired."
Enkidu spoke to Gilgamesh, saying:
        "It is true, there are many days left in us,
        these people are already tired."

Gilgamesh spoke, saying:
        "We are both great warriors, you and I Enkidu,
        but I am the king.
        There can be no defeat for me.
Enkidu spoke, saying:

"It is true, we are both great warriors, you and I
      Gilgamesh,
but you bring great grief to these people.
There can be no defeat for me.

The two waged their war again,
the people of Uruk-Haven began to cry out.

Gilgamesh spoke to Enkidu, saying:
      I was wrong to steal from these people, Enkidu,
      I was seeking something they did not have.
      I was not being a wise king, but instead a selfish king.
      My people do not know this,
      they do not understand as you understand Enkidu,
      for you and I are alike."
Enkidu said to Gilgamesh:
      "Your mother bore a great and unique son.
      You are truly a wise king.
      Your strength is the mightiest in the land!"

Enkidu raised his voice to the people of Uruk:
      Gilgamesh's strength is the mightiest in the land,
      his strength is as mighty as the Meterorite of Anu,
      he is a good and wise king."

The two kissed each other and became friends.
The mother of Gilgamesh spoke to Gilgamesh, saying;
Rimat-Ninsun said to her son:
      "I, Rimat-Ninsun, your mother, understand.
      My son, these three days were your three dreams.
      Enkidu has acquiesced to you my son, but he is not
          vanquished,
      do not banish this worthy challenger as you should
          by custom."
She went up into Shamash's gateway, and said:

"Enkidu has no father or mother,
his shaggy hair no one cuts.
He was born in the wilderness, no one raised him."

Enkidu was standing there, and heard the speech.
He staggered and sat down and wept,
his eyes filled with tears,
his arms felt limp, his strength weakened.

Gilgamesh and Enkidu took each other by the hand,
and with their hands woven into each other's like one
the two walked to the palace.

From the Author

Given the nature of poetry in general, and postmodern poetry specifically, the providing of fair attribution for creations partly gleened from the minds of others is often artistically impossible, … and, I might add, generally absurd.

As an artist though, I would, from the very depths of my heart and soul, like to thank the artistic "mentors" that had a profound influence on my work captured on these pages. Thank you to Pablo Neruda, Pablo Picasso, Dylan Thomas, Hans Küng, James Joyce, Charles Mingus, The Kronos Quartet, Noam Chomsky, Umberto Eco, Ludwig von Beethoven, Ludwig Feuerbach, Sylvia Plath, Henri Poincaré, Jorge Luis Borges, Michel Foucault, Friedrich Nietzsche, Albert Einstein, Rainer Maria Rilke, Theodor Adorno, John Coltrane, John Cage, Edward Lorenz, and Thorstein Veblen. Thank you also to Maureen Gallery Kovacs for her wonderful translation of the Epic of Gilgamesh from which I liberally drew to craft this piece which I consider to, in many ways, be my own translation of the first two tablets of the epic.

Christopher Johnston

Christopher Johnston is a Senior Research Fellow at the Center for Alternative Studies in Peace and Social Justice where he heads the Center's Middle East Project.